UNSEEN
TREASURES

Embrace the Message Within

Darlene Garland & Francillia Foublasse

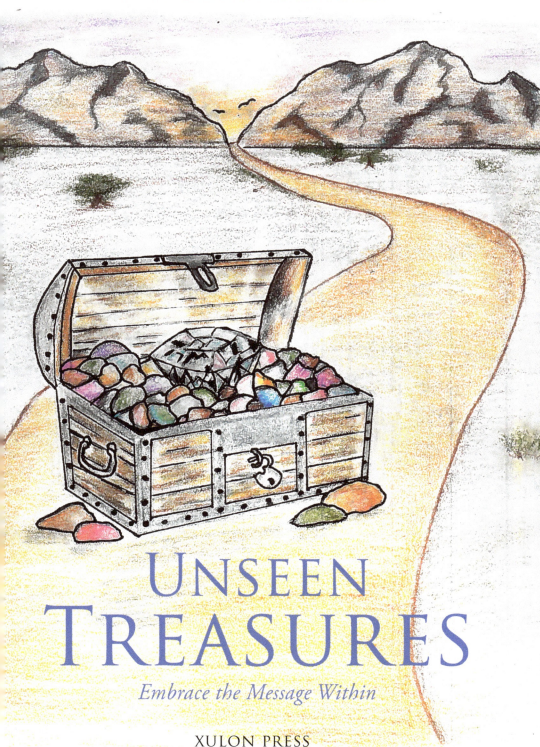

Unseen Treasures

Embrace the Message Within

XULON PRESS

Xulon Press
2301 Lucien Way #415
Maitland, FL 32751
407.339.4217
www.xulonpress.com

Paperback ISBN-13: 978-1-66285-491-0
Ebook ISBN-13: 978-1-66285-492-7

DEDICATIONS

DARLENE'S DEDICATION:

To my one in a million husband, Cedric. Thank you for all the love, support, and for always believing in me when I didn't believe in myself. We did it! I love doing life with you. – *Your loving wife.*

To my beloved sister, Clarita Mays. Although our plans to write a book together will never be, I took your advice to slow down and embrace love, family, life, nature, and appreciate the present. Living in the present state of gratitude sharpens my awareness of God's creation. God speaks at all times, this time it was through rocks! You are dearly missed. – *Your baby sister, Doll.*

To my Prayer Warrior Sister, Cill. You are truly a gift from God, and I treasure you. Our divine connection years ago has developed into one of the most precious gifts of friendship and sisterhood. God knew my desire to write a book with my sister, and He took us on a journey together. Forever grateful. – *Prayer Warrior Sister, Darlene.*

FRANCILLIA'S DEDICATION:

Life takes us through many journeys with those that are seasonal and those that are permanently assigned to teach and guide us to our full potential. In appreciation of all the lessons learned along the way, I thank my many teachers. My personal dedication to this assignment of love goes to my saving grace, Jesus Christ. In addition, I dedicate my growth in the process to my children, Julian, Amber, and Jordan.

Thank you, Darlene, for agreeing to work on this together with me and putting our hearts in the direction that the Lord so purposed. You entrusted to me your desire to work with your sister, Clarita and I believe this is an extension of her love for you. Let us truly embrace the journey of God's joy. — *Francillia (AKA Your sister, Cill)*

ACKNOWLEDGMENT

Our acknowledgment goes to our Lord and Savior, Jesus Christ, without whom, this project of love would not be possible. We would further like to thank our families and friends for their support and love along the way.

CONTENTS

PREFACE

*U*nseen Treasures has been structured in such a manner that allows the reader to read from front to back or skip around without missing the point of the book. Our obligation is for you to be reflective throughout the reading. We have chosen to elaborate from our individual frame of mind when writing, as we discuss main sources, thereby offering our perspective upon the completed work. This book is a project of love, in which we examine by a variety of symbols from our findings during our enlightened walks and our appreciation goes to the *unknown artist*.

The various symbols, characters, examples, and storylines start with an immense appreciation of the captured symbolic messages along with Biblical references to expand upon the depth of our spiritual connections. Core themes will always circle back to our Almighty creator including individual imaginations and or experiences. Our purpose in writing this book is to remind our friends, our readers, that God often appears in our complicated situations, and He is present also in the simple details of our daily life.

We acknowledge our referenced source, the Bible, paying reverence to our Magnificent Advocate, the Holy Spirit, as we capture our experiences. We were reminded, inspired, motivated, and challenged, through the journaling of this writing; we thank you for becoming a part of our collective and connective journey.

INTRODUCTION

The Garland family was hosting yet another set of guests, myself included, in their love-filled home. It was a beautiful day in October, the sun was shining, a light breeze of wind was blowing, the birds were chirping, and the trees were responding to their Creator in perfect harmony. It seemed like no one was in a hurry, even the cars were not racing down the street. If one paused for a moment to take it all in, the awesomeness of God could momentarily be described by our limited understanding. Just a perfect morning to start our day.

We had taken walks before, but today something was different, there was a special magic in the air. There was a thankfulness about the Earth. We were doing our usual customary talks about life and sharing our experiences with each other. We could have easily missed it, but something caught my attention. "Hey, what is that over there?" I asked my walking partner, Darlene. In mid-conversation, we paused to examine what had caught the eye.

"What is it?" We proceeded to take a closer look and to our delight, we had discovered an awesome treasure.

Semi-hidden amongst the bush and rocks, it seemed to almost look back at us, a rock with an image on it. On the painted rock was a symbol of a pink flamingo standing on one leg. Interesting we thought, "Who would paint this beautiful symbol on a rock and leave it there?" Perhaps it had fallen from someone, and they lost their beautiful painted rock.

I wondered, should we take it? Was it a message for us? Were there more of these around? We checked around but did not find any additional painted rocks. Forgetting what we were previously discussing, we admired the artwork displayed on that rock and let it speak to our individual hearts. Tempted to possess it, we contemplated our options; should we take it, or leave it for others to discover? Was it meant only for us? We wanted very much to keep it but we reasoned someone else might appreciate it too, or even the owner may be looking for it.

Our discussion took a turn as we marveled at the mysteries of God and how much we are loved by him. We started to share how much God has shown up in our lives over the years even when we were not fully aware of his goodness. We concluded what a fantastic ministry to have, to be able to leave a message of hope for complete strangers along the path of this artistic journey. We found three additional rocks that morning and admired and reflected on the meaning each imparted.

Unbeknownst to each other at the time, our minds were spinning as each in our reflective thought wondered how we too can contribute to the positive message found on those rocks. The ideas in this book was the result of those reflective thoughts, how wonderful it would be to extend this artist's work by tying it to the Biblical treasures of old and new.

We were simply taking a morning stroll, and something caught our eye. Here, we were discussing God in nature, and just like that, He appeared in the very elements of our discussion: ROCKS!!!! It reminded us of the story of Peter when Jesus stated, upon this rock, I will build my church. No, Jesus was not talking about Peter (the man), but of himself. The Rock was a representation of him who Peter had declared to be the Christ, the Son of the Living God.

Many treasures of hope were discovered that day simply because we stopped, looked, observed, and learned from the planted treasures along our path. We found a half dozen rocks of hope over the next few mornings and were as excited as little kids to increase our treasure box. We were tempted to keep each rock we discovered, but reasoning got the best of us because we wanted others to be as excited as we were when they too came across those messages of hope.

We believed God was reminding us that sharing is caring and based on the level of excitement we each received with our discovery, others would likewise experience their own joy. With childlike curiosity, we made it our purpose that day to find more treasures, from that day onwards. When we look to find God and make him a treasure within our life, He will indeed fulfill our heart's desires.

We started to see God, our creator, in everything that day. It became so real in our mind's eye. We too wanted to start painting and writing on rocks and leaving them in our neighborhoods. We wanted to do more! We wanted to let the artist know how much their work was accomplished, how much it was touching lives, how much they were making a difference, how remarkable this project was, how much God was coming alive to us, and we assumed to others as well.

Our idea led to this collaborative book project in which we would use pictures to share the teachings of God, through scriptures, and expound on the messages from the rocks of hope. We wanted to bring out the simplicity of the messages with a tangible connection to our God, the one who sees and knows everything. We wanted the artist to know that their work was not in vain, and it was having a positive impact on the lives of others, specifically our own. Although we have no clue who this person is, we know that nothing is impossible with God, He can find a way to make this book known to the artist, the inspiration to our book idea.

In the journey of life, may you see with your physical eyes, but be enlightened with the eye of your heart, your spiritual eye. May God, our creator, open your eyes into the supernatural. May you take the journey of your created purpose to shed a light on others. May you find beyond the challenges of life the simplicity of the joy that can be found in the hope of creation. May all life lessons land you in a place of loving reflection. May you too find the elements that make a difference in your journey, the factors that bring eternal deliverance. May you see the exclamation in the beauty of this life. May you find our God, the only one that can fulfill and seal the void in your heart. May the messages ahead be exactly what you are looking for and may God bring true satisfaction to your heart's desires.

And as stated in the priestly blessings to the children of Israel from our God in *Numbers 6:24-26 (NIV)*: *"The Lord bless you and keep you; the Lord make his face shine on you and be gracious to you; the Lord turn his face toward you and give you peace."*

Remember to keep an open heart. There are many messages that God reveals to us when we need them the most and there is much more than what the eye can see. God is continuously speaking to us. Take heart beloved and may God grant you the eye to see yourself in the stories and treasures that lies ahead. As you reflect on the messages, internalize them as if God had selected the content just for you.

Chapter 1

RARE AND BEAUTIFUL

I like to enjoy my quiet time on walking paths. Somedays I would go around my block a few times, other times I walk through the parks in my neighborhood, or just through the surrounding areas. I do not have any certain pace in walking nor any time limit. As I walk, I like to stop and observe my surrounding, pray, sing, and listen to God and the birds.

One day while walking, I had seen among many rocks something that caught my attention. A colorful purple rock with some bold writing. I approached it with anticipation and was curious to read the wording. As I bent down to pick up the rock the message in bold dark black letters "you are rare and beautiful." I felt an overflowing feeling of love. Some heaviness inside of me that I was unaware of lifted. My spirit became lighter, and I felt happy. I did not think I was feeling any certain way, but the message on the rock lifted my spirit.

Reading you are rare and beautiful from a stranger really ministered to me. Even the thought of a stranger unselfishly taking time to encourage another stranger brought hope and a smile. I felt hope knowing there are people out there that care for someone else besides themselves. I felt hope knowing that someone wanted to make a difference in someone else's life in a small way via this rock. On that day, I knew I was that someone. The purple rock with "you are rare and beautiful" was meant for me to read.

I hope many others have seen and took the time to read it. I believe the message encouraged, ignited, and reminded every reader to be the change in the world they want to see. If no one has seen it besides me, at least I am doing something about what I have seen and felt.

Immediately, I felt an obligation to reevaluate my life, action, and any lack of action that hinders me from being or becoming beautiful and rare. I took a moment to receive all the rock had to offer me and placed it back down in eyesight view for anyone else who will be walking or running to see and embrace the impact of the kind and encouraging words as I did that day.

In fact, thinking back on those words still resonate my spirit. I felt it was a sign from God telling me that I matter. You matter as well. In the Bible *Psalm 139 (NIV)* mentions we are *'fearfully and wonderfully made'* in His image. God intimately knows every person and all humanity belongs to Him. This means from the womb to the tomb everyone is in

His image. Take a moment and sit in that thought. Amazing, is it not? He is amazing, and you are amazing!

Have you ever heard those words before? If not, can you fully recognize and accept the impact they can have on your life? To be fearfully and wonderfully made in His image. He created and designed each person with a purpose. We are similar because we are human beings, yet rare and beautiful individually.

I often wonder, had anyone else seen that purple rock as they were walking or running? Did anyone stop to read the message? What was their reaction after reading it? Did the message resonate with them as it did with me? Did they just see it as a rock with some words on it and went about their walk/ run? How did and has it impacted their life, their thoughts about themselves and their reality?

If we only take the time to listen and watch, God softly speaks to us daily through people, objects, nature, and situations. There are many reasons why we miss hearing, seeing, or knowing His voice or disregarding our God moments.

I can honestly admit that I do not always lean in to hear, look for Him, or at times know for sure if it is really Him. But I am certain on that day He wanted to get my attention to remind me of who He created me to be. You may wonder, how do I know for sure? He is all-knowing of everything we think or do before we realize it. Purple is one of my favorite colors.

As you continue to read, you will understand why purple is one of the colors of the rainbow analyzed. Whenever I see purple, doesn't matter what it is, it gets my full attention and I respond. The purple rock got my attention which caused me to stop, listen, and respond. Yes, all this from walking, finding, reading, and receiving the message from a purple rock. Let me share a few things about me.

God created us uniquely, in which we all have our own DNA (Deoxyribonucleic Acid). He knows everything about us including our likes and dislikes. Yes, He knows every thought before we speak it. In *Jeremiah 1:5 (ESV): "Before I formed you in the womb, I knew you, and before you were born, I consecrated you; I appointed you a prophet to the nations"* Therefore, you cannot hide the so-called good, bad, or the ugly from Him. He is all-knowing. He knows what pulls our heartstrings even when we do not know or understand them.

A second thought that came into my mind after reading the word "rare" on the purple rock was, "I am one of a kind created in this world." There is no one else like me. To fully explain that feeling without giving the perception of pride or arrogance is challenging. As part of our understanding of the impactful meaning of being "rare" the way God created you, you need to first embrace self-love.

You may be wondering what exactly self-love is. I am referring to nurturing the perspective of oneself in a loving way. Self-love is becoming aware of your flaws or shortcoming in a lovely way and making a conscious decision to improve in those areas. You may be aware of things in your life that need to be changed, added to, or gotten rid of, to achieve a better version of yourself. If you are unaware of such, ask a trusted person and give them permission to speak the truth over you. Accept their honest opinion, be open to take self-inventory, and do not try to justify your actions. Just listen and later quietly get by yourself to do a hardcore reality check on self-evaluation. Pray and meditate about what and how to do all that you need to do. As painful as it may become, nothing of value comes without a price. Commit and know the overall benefits you will achieve through effort and time. If you do not invest in and love yourself, no one else will. Knowing your worth is "rare."

It is rare among many people to know and recognize their worth to self, their family, and others their paths cross. I am a firm believer that when one knows better there should be some effort on their part to do better. In *James 4:17 (NKJV): "Therefore to him who knows to do good and does not do it, to him it is sin."* There are times in life we may want to do better or good, but our sinful and selfish nature takes over our better judgment. It is not always about money, prestige, titles, or competing with others. It is about striving for happiness, peace, fulfillment, and being content no matter the circumstances.

It is rare to know your strengths and weakness without becoming ashamed or arrogant. It is not easy to embrace and accept where you are at the present and yet move toward becoming even greater. Many people may love themselves, but do not like who they become. I can honestly say I know people who love and appreciate others over themselves. Sadly, they cannot grasp nor comprehend their value of themselves. They rather believe the lies that were told to them by themselves or others. The comparison or beliefs of others that they set for themselves is unattainable in their sight. Yet more than likely they are within their reach but their low self-esteem, lack of confidence, or just stinky things prevent them from thinking differently. I hope you recognize the worth and value you bring to the world. You must recognize yourself as worthy and still have a humble spirit.

I think of self-love as being my own best friend. The same way I treasure friendship, I care and love myself enough to be authentic with who I have become. I am protective of myself in establishing safe boundaries. I guard my heart and try to nurture my mind through positive self-talk. I pray, meditate, and surround my home with words of affirmation to encourage and keep my sanity. Please realize you must do whatever you need to do to treasure and value who you are, no matter how crazy it may be to others. You are worth the cost, time, and effort. Being rare is always going the extra mile when others slack up, hold back, or quit.

Being "rare" should put a different perspective on how you should view yourself. As mentioned earlier beauty can be compared and valued through the eyes of the beholder. Rare is authentic and can always be traced back to the original. Just like every individual can be identified and traced back through their individual fingerprints. It amazes me that even identical twins have different fingerprints.

Although twins or multiples have the same genetic characteristics that may cause difficulty in recognizing them outwardly, not everything is exactly alike. There may be quite a few similarities in appearances, personalities, likes, dislikes to name a few. Importantly, they are and should be considered as individuals with a life of their own to live out separately.

I ponder over the thought of what makes a person rare. Can an individual be defined as rare? What makes an individual stand out or be recognized by others to be so different that the word "rare" comes to mind?

The Bible mentions everyone is created in the image of God. We all should reflect Him in our character. *Galatians 5 (NIV)* mentions the fruit of the Spirit is *love, joy, peace, forbearance, kindness, goodness, faithfulness, gentleness, and self-control*; against such things, there is no law. These attributes complete the fruit of the spirit. If all these attributes are present, then you are exhibiting the whole fruit of the spirit. There is no such thing as a partial fruit of the spirit. In other words, it is all or nothing.

Unfortunately, not very often do people display the full spectrum of the fruit of the spirit. Many can display a few qualities of the fruit in certain situations or toward different people. Many can love, have joy, and show kindness toward their immediate family, personal friends, and whomever they like. Yet are impatient, harsh, evil with no self-control toward strangers, co-workers, or anyone they dislike.

People are considered rare when they can demonstrate the full fruit of the Spirit toward everyone and in all situations. In *Mark 12:30-31 (NIV): "Love the Lord your God with all your heart and with all your soul and with all your mind and with all your strength. The second is this: Love your neighbor as yourself. There is no commandment greater than these."*

Most people have become distrusting and suspicious of one another actions or intentions. Loving your fellow man or woman just because the Bible teaches us, is not easy. Love your neighbor as yourself is even harder. I realize many people do not fully love themselves making it extremely difficult for them to love someone especially outside of their immediate circle.

Nowadays, it may seem strange when being loving, positive, having integrity, helping others without wanting anything back in return is considered rare. Even a simple action as opening a door for someone to go ahead of you or holding it for the person behind you, smiling to acknowledge someone, speaking to strangers, or just being kind is considered rare.

Within the fruit of the spirit is faithfulness. There are many people in the Bible that their faithfulness would be considered rare. Their devotion, willingness, trust, faith, belief, love, and actions testify to being rare. They stood out among others during Biblical times and are examples for us today. God used them because He knew their heart and trusted their faithfulness.

Noah was a righteous man, blameless among people of his time. He found favor in the eyes of the Lord. *(Genesis 6:8-10 NIV)*

Samuel as a child minister before God was considered faithful *(1 Samuel 2:26, 1 Samuel 3: 1-20 and Jeremiah 15:1 NIV)*

David was a faithful priest to God and a faithful son-in-law to King Saul *(1 Samuel 2:35 and 1 Samuel 22:14 NIV)*

Lydia, a new convert, was faithful to Paul and Timothy, and they stayed at her house along with her household *(Acts 16:14-16 NIV)*

God considered Paul to be faithful and put him in the ministry *(1 Timothy 1:12 NIV)*

Yet the ultimate epitome of rare is Jesus Christ. His sacrifice and love for us are rare to mankind. If we study His life journey from birth to resurrection, we will find out there is no other whose life is so perfect yet so loving and caring. There will never be anyone like Him. But His love causes us to desire His image.

How can someone be rare while others are a dime a dozen? Is being rare something that a person works to become or is it inborn? Do people strive and make a conscious decision to be a different from the majority? Does being authentic make you rare? What stands out above or uniquely? It is easy to mistake rare with being familiar just because one may think they know or have many similarities, fake copies, but nothing like the original?

The word rare brings to mind famous artwork and precious jewels. But not even an artist can paint a perfectly identical copy of their own masterpiece. An artist's signature either on the front or back of their work is proof of original. Expert in authentic studies can recognize original work through signature, technique, texture, material, and even the uniqueness of the brush stroke. The workmanship is rare or valuable because of the limited quantity.

The challenge for many people to believe or understand God is because this world has distorted the simplest, yet purest emotion called "Love". Pure love has no boundaries, reaches past all barriers, has no limitations or conditions. It can be felt and expressed by everyone and every creature. Love is a deep inward emotion that expresses itself through an outward response.

As mentioned throughout these pages God created us in His image. *Ephesians 2:10 (NIV)* mentions *"For we are God's handiwork, created in Christ Jesus to do good works, which God prepared in advance for us to do."*

It may be hard to believe everyone born is on their individual journey. This journey comes together like pieces of a puzzle with everyone fitting perfectly together for the glory of God. In *Jeremiah 1:5 (NIV)* we read, *"Before I formed you in the womb, I knew you, before you were born, I set you apart; I appointed you as a prophet to the nations."* He knew us before conception and gave everyone specific earthly parents to birth us into the world for His Glory and Great Commission.

The Great Commission is to spread the news of Him to people throughout the nations and the world. To be willing to tell others about His love, death, and resurrection and to become followers. Many people think they need to be perfect or close to it to become a follower or take part in the Great Commission. This is far from the truth. It is as simple as A-B-C; *A* to *Accept* Jesus into your heart as your personal Savior; *Believe* He died on a cross for your sins and arose from the dead and then *Confess* your sins to Him and know that they are forgiven.

Doing these steps with true repentance and by faith receiving Him into your heart as your Lord and Savior immediately one makes you a follower. Yes, it is just that simple. Simple enough that no one is exempt from becoming a follower. In trusting the process as a follower, one becomes a disciple with the desire to tell others about Him.

Are you wondering, "Who is a disciple?" A disciple of Christ is someone who believes in the Word of God, lives it, and teaches others to become followers as well. The words follower and believer are interchangeable terminologies. Once I accepted Him into my heart, I wanted to know about Him and how He felt about me. I found out more by reading the Bible, hearing other followers tell their personal experiences, and praying. I felt loved and at peace, which I could not totally understand. I realized Jesus gave His all for me and promises to never leave me. His presence is always with me. He loves me unconditionally. He created me to be rare and unique. My heart desire wanted others even strangers to accept Him into their lives.

When you accept Christ into your life you believe by faith, your perceptive changes to wanting to be more like Him. Hopefully, an unselfish nature turns the heart toward Him. His love and grace for you transfer to wanting others to experience a personal relationship with Him too.

In *Matthew 28: 18-20 (NKJV)* we read, *'"And Jesus came and spoke to them, saying, 'All authority has been given to Me in heaven and on earth. Go therefore and make disciples of all the nations, baptizing them in the name of the Father and of the Son and of the Holy Spirit, teaching them to observe all things that I have commanded you; and lo, I am with you always even to the end of the ages. Amen."'* When you accept Christ into your life you believe, follow, and want to live by the guidelines in the Bible.

Acts 2:36-38 (NIV) gives a scriptural view of baptism; to be baptized in Christ is having your whole body immersed in water as a representation of purging old sinful self, dying with Christ, and coming out cleanse in Christ. Once you have done your earthly commitment to become a follower, the real test of your faith begins. You have proclaimed to the world that God exists and is governor over your life. That the freewill He has given you, you willingly turn it over to Him. You have confessed that He knows all about you and created you therefore you return yourself back to Him. Now your journey begins. There is earthly confession to live by, follow, teach, and train others to do the same.

God has unconditional love for each of us. His love has no boundaries. He is unlike most of us when it comes to love or loving someone. Most people seem to love others with emotions or under conditions. If one does not live up to their expectations their love for them changes. If this is the case, you should question that kind of love it was in the beginning. His love is not an emotional rollercoaster. For God so loved the world that He willingly gave His only Son for us. He knew we will fail at times and are sinful people but by giving His Son in replacement for our sins we can be with Him for eternity. God sees us through love and the shed blood of His Son.

On that day I did not have any idea how, when, or if I was going to hear from God but He knew I needed to have an encounter with Him. He knew I would decide to take that specific walking path. Let me go even deeper because He is in the details: He had a stranger pick the right size rock, painted purple, gave the words to write, and placed the rock in the right location at the perfect time for me to see.

He is precise in the very details to get our attention. His plans do not fall out of the sky, not that it cannot. Sometimes He uses people to participate in delivering a message to us. That one is no secret, He does it all the time, think about it, have you ever been thinking of a person, and they called, text, or send a message to you at that very moment? Yes, God is in the details of our life.

In *Psalm 37:4 (NKJV)* says *"Delight yourself also in the LORD, And He shall give you the desires of your heart."* You may have heard the expression, 'we are His hands and feet.' Not that He needs us because He is God, but we get the privilege of playing a small part in His purpose for us. He loves us that much to want a personal relationship with us. I am so grateful and thankful for that opportunity to work with God.

The purple color reminds me of strength, royalty, very pleasing to my eyes, and brings up memories. Many of my loved ones liked the color as well. Since many of them are no longer here, the purple color brings me in remembrance of them. Who would have thought a color can spark an emotion? God knew! He created our 5 senses to respond and react to our surroundings.

I feel both statements "beauty is in the eyes of the beholder" and "beauty is skin deep" are true. Beauty is in the eyes of the beholder is more of the outer appearance or something that is pleasing to the eye. Beauty is more than a perception an individual person perceives about themselves. If we take the time to look around, beauty surrounds us.

Have you ever looked at the sun rise, how it bursts through the sky with a bright orange shining crystal ball? I am always fascinated by the God's creation and the radiant colors that bring pleasure to the eyes.

The snowcapped mountain top and how it stands high with the breath-taking blue skies behind it. The beauty of the different forms of the mountains each has its own unique shape, groove, foliage, and span. The mountains represent the quest for the knowledge of God, the pinnacle of achievement or the curse of defeat. God often told the children of Israel to come up the mountain of the Lord and have encounters and communion with Him. *Judges 5:5 (NASV)* states, *"The mountains quaked at the presence of the Lord, This Sinai, at the presence of the Lord, the God of Israel."*

Man must take what already exists to do what God has already done before. Have you ever thought, if man knows so much why haven't life been created (or recreated) through dirt or taken from another person's rib like at the beginning of time? Why has man's ability not outperformed that of God, despite our intellect? Just a thought.

The beauty of a newborn baby. The encounter or hearing the cry for the first time from the first breath being birthed into this world is mind blowing. Seeing those tiny fingers and toes, the newness of it all. The beauty of a woman carrying a little human in her body for nine months. Why nine? Why not another number? Because while the number Biblically represents the finality, it is divine completeness, three times three, as in the trinity of the spirit, soul, and body. Man represents the image of God, created in his image for his purpose. Yes, man can explain the process of birth, but only God created life in His image.

The beauty of how an individual perceives themselves or accepts the opinions of others as either negative or positive impacts their self-esteem. As a child, I remember the saying that sticks and stones that break my bones, but names will never hurt me. In reality, 'name calling' does hurt especially names that lower your self-esteem. We hear first impressions are important. Do not let anyone fool you, the first appearance is also important, as a first impression can define you without even opening your mouth. It can work for or against you, we are in a culture of making impressions of each other, good or bad.

Our eye gate sends a message to the brain which forms an opinion. I believe most people want their first impression to be likeable. They may feel being physically attractive can help in many incidents to serve as an advance. And sadly, in our worldly culture that is often the case. As a result, I believe unconsciously we all want to be looked upon as beautiful. Some people allow others to tell or confirm that they are "beautiful".

The purple rock was appealing to me, and the words written expressed its beauty toward me. We all make this judgment daily. Thank God, we can worship a God who defines us all as beautiful, each undeserving of His goodness and mercy, but provided to us regardless of our individual makeup. We are created in His image for His purpose.

The Merriam Webster Thesaurus defines beautiful as pleasing the senses or mind aesthetically. The synonyms of beautiful are attractive, pretty, handsome, good looking, nice looking, of an extremely high standard, or excellent. I would add that being beautiful is not always an outer appearance. I believe beauty can be an inward expression as well.

An inward expression that adds to confidence, raises your self-esteem and can make you feel beautiful. When you have His joy there is an inside smile that makes you radiant on the outside. The beauty you feel when someone gives you a compliment, only you can react to it. The area or spot that pulls you up or brightens your day. A person can allow others to make them feel beautiful or do some self-care loving of themselves. Personally, I prefer the latter. Taking care of your needs whenever you want giving to yourself is more beneficial.

Frankly, you do not have to rely on someone treating you or giving you what you can do for yourself. You should feel beautiful when pampering yourself. Some external gestures include buying a good smelling perfume, treating yourself to a cute outfit, soaking in a warm bathtub, relaxing, rubbing your body with nice smelling body lotion, spending time with yourself, taking a well-deserved trip, soaking in His presence, etc. We all are unique individuals, no one should be allowed to dictate what makes you feel beautiful or what you perceive as beautiful. I hope your takeaway is that we are all created to be fearfully and wonderfully made, each unique.

The same goes for the perception of beauty. In saying this, I do not believe there is any place on earth where we are not affected by outer appearance. Unfortunately, that is the state of the world; we have been conditioned by the external factors that can consume our thoughts and mental assessment. Yes, we can blame it on the media, commercials, upbringing, and other opinions. It is hard maybe impossible to change or disregard the ways, thoughts, voices, looks, perceptions on that subject. Regardless of those conditions, nothing is impossible with God.

He desires to change our hearts and minds towards His purpose. No one could ever live up to the false images or maintain them for long, that life is exhausting. Hopefully, once we accept our individuality, that we are created differently with our own likes, dislikes, and opinions, those of others should not matter as much. That is the beauty of being rare and beautiful.

Psalm 139 (NIV) mentions we are "fearfully and wonderfully made". I find it sad that many people resent the beauty that God has given to them. He has given us beauty among people, objects, nature, and relationships. Beauty is not always the outer appearance of a person nor the exterior of a material thing, such as a mansion. If one would take the time, you will find beauty surrounds us daily with our natural and supernatural eyes.

Yes, beauty in the eye of the beholder can come from waking up in the morning with the attitude of gratitude. There is beauty through a sunrise or sunset, formation of clouds in the sky, fancy sports car, a kiss from a loved one, snow peak mountaintop, encouraging words, or even a painted rock.

Beautiful can become a curse when it's to be the standard upon which one weighs life with or use it the manipulation of people and circumstances.

Have you ever been mistaken or allowed your eyes to define what is beautiful on the outside did not line up with the ugliness that is displayed on the inside? The inside overshadows the first impression of the outside which caused being ugly throughout. This goes back to the saying beauty is only skin deep.

Lucifer was known as a beautiful fallen angel. Even evil appears to be beautiful on the outside. In *Ezekiel 28: 17 (NIV): "Your heart became proud on account of your beauty, and you corrupted your wisdom because of your splendor."*

In many ways, the saying 'smiling faces' show no traces of the evil that alerts within is a reality. Most people rely on the outer attractiveness of a person to be their meter to approach or let their guard down. We all should approach people and situations with a grain of salt. Do not just listen to words but watch their actions. The Bible says it this way, *Matthew 7:15-16 (KJV) "Be aware of false prophets, which come to you in sheep's clothing, but inwardly they are ravenous wolves. Ye shall know them by their fruits."* You may be wondering what false prophets and fruit have to do with being beautiful. I believe to a certain degree people who exhibit a tendency of a respecter of others look at outward actions only and not the totality of being.

The Bible lays out a beautiful example in the story of Esther relating to both internal and external beauty. In the story of Esther, we learned that the young virgins who were being prepared to be presented before the king took the rarity and beauty of the process. The process itself took a total of one year to be exact, which consisted of six months anointing themselves with oil such as myrrh and another six months with additional products for purification.

During this time process, the Bible records that Esther found favor with everyone who looked upon her, the favor of man, often due to external factors. Esther also had the favor of God, internal beauty. Esther was both rare and beautiful, as beauty is indeed in the eyes of the beholder. Both God and man looked upon Esther with favor.

This story grabbed my attention as I often think of God as a just God, and my limited view wants to say that Esther had an advantage relative to others. But did she? God always has a plan, and it will be fulfilled. God asks of man, in assisting with his plan, is for us to obey. He reminds us that obedience is better than sacrifice.

Queen Vashti (Esther's predecessor) could have been the one to carry out God's plan, the Bible does not elaborate on this, only that Queen Vashti chose to disobey when requested by the king to appear before his quests. As a result, she was removed from the palace. Having been removed from the palace, the plan of God was still in effect, to save the children of Abraham, Isaac, and Jacob...the Israelites. Since women are the gateway to the kingdom of God, the plan continued with Queen Esther.

History will show us that most of the fall of man, has a woman at the base, beginning with Adam in the book of Genesis. But also of interesting highlights are the fact that God often used a woman to align with His will in fulfilling appointed plans. Many of such women included Deborah, Ruth, Rahab, Mary, Lydia, Priscilla, and yes Esther, the focus of our discussion.

I believe God choosing a woman to save the Jewish people was a reconciliation of sorts. A precursor of Jesus who would come through the virgin Mary to reconcile God's people unto himself. It required the obedience of Mary to say, 'be it unto me according to your word' for her to give birth to our Lord Jesus, who would be the Savior necessary for the continuation of God's people.

Women are gateways into the reconciliation unto God. Esther likewise had to agree in obedience for the fulfillment of God's plan. God will never force man to obey Him but will give us the courage to do so, once we have chosen Him. Like Joshua stated, "choose this day, whom you will serve… as for me and my household we will serve the Lord." *Joshua 24:15 (ESV).*

Esther was hesitant to carry out such a task, but thankfully she had her uncle Mordecai to both encourage her and remind her of her purpose. He told her, 'Who knows if you had been created and assigned to this task for such a time as this.' Hearing this, Esther told her uncle Mordecai if I perish, I perish!

Jesus also had His moment in the Garden of Gethsemane and asked the Father, "was there any other way to accomplish his purpose?" Thankfully, Jesus said, "'nevertheless', not my will but your will be done." We too will feel it impossible for the task and purpose we have been created to do, let me encourage you to find your 'nevertheless'; your 'if I perish, I perish' moments. We, too, have an assistant, the Holy Spirit who lives in us. The Holy Spirit was provided to be our helper, our advocate, our support system, our guide, our teacher, and our consciousness to our next essential step, may we harken to the Spirit today.

Our God has promised us to never leave us nor forsake us, not that we would not encounter trials and tribulations. As a matter of fact, Jesus stated in this life we would have many trials and tribulations, but be not discouraged, he has overcome them all, (paraphrase, *John 16:33 (KJV))*. Esther was uncertain about her instructions but still chose to obey despite the fear and the potential death that would result. Her inner beauty prevailed on behalf of her people, she chose to follow the instructions and even called a fast to hear with clarity the voice of God. We have a beautiful example in the life of Esther when we make our decision to live for God.

God has perfect timing, in this story, we learned of his timing, even down to the details of God opening the opportunity for the king to receive Esther and hear her plea. When we are tempted to get discouraged, remember God is in the details, trust the process.

Interesting fact, the word "God" was never mentioned in the book of Esther, but it has the signs of God all over it in the many details. If we look around, we see signs of God everywhere; in nature, in others, in situations, in disappointments, in trials, in energy, in the things that work out for our good, in the things that do not work now but gets delayed or a no, in multiple facets of life. God is everywhere, the Earth is the Lord's. God has promised to give us beauty for our ashes. Remember, *"For all the promises of God in him are yea, and in him Amen, unto the glory of God by us."* – *2 Corinthians 1:20 (KJV)*, now that is a beautiful promise!

The beauty of the life God has given all of us is unknown to the number of years. The beauty of it is that we have a choice on how to live out our days in the elements of God's graces. The freedom of choice on how that plays out is our own decision or some may say, the making of our faith.

Our freewill requires that we get to decide. It did cost the Father to provide us that freewill. Jesus paid the ultimate cost on the cross for all of us. Our true freedom comes with the acceptance of Jesus' death and resurrection. Every decision or action comes with a price or sacrifice. We have been bought with the precious blood of Jesus into our freedom.

We all have only one life to live here on earth and each passing day draws us closer to our death. As believers, that is our true freedom, death is our separation into eternity. On the other hand, it is also the separation from God if we have chosen not to accept the gift of eternity. We all have 24 hours in a day to choose how to live it. The real beauty comes when you realize how precious life really is. Hopefully, this realization will cause us not to waste precious and nonreturnable moments on unimportant things. Hopefully, it will help you prioritize your life by putting first things first, the Kingdom of God.

As a young kid, I used to hear my parents and older adults say things like "quit wasting time it will get away from you sooner than you think, you need to start thinking about life and what you want to do, before you know it you are too old to do anything," or "Don't live life with any regrets." "Time will come sooner than you think." Most young people think they have plenty of time as the clock ticks away. Having come to a stage of maturity, most of us wish we knew then what we know now.

The beauty is when you figure out early on and strive towards that in your calling in life to be successful. It will indeed be beautiful. Make this world a better place and then do reach back, out, sideways, and down to bring someone else along to experience the rarity of that beauty. We are called to support each other, but to be that supporter you must position yourself in life to be that person who values self-care so that others who depend on you can be positively impacted.

Be that rock with encouraging words, helping hands and an open heart. Life is a journey with many paths, the beauty is enjoying it with someone, experiencing joy with others, and hearing about someone else successes, even a perfect stranger. Beauty is when you can share in someone else's happiness, success of fulfillment, and accomplishments. The real beauty that shines from within and outward is when you can generously be happy for someone without any benefit or ulterior motives on your end.

Observation Point: Can you sit in this thought? Can you be happy for someone that achieved more than you? Can you have an open heart to be authentic without envy or jealousy? If so, this is what I call endearing, which is both rare and beautiful.

Reader's Notes: *Embrace the Message Within*

_____

_____

_____

_____

_____

_____

_____

_____

_____

_____

_____

_____

_____

Chapter 2
GOPHER

What is that? Is it a squirrel, a rodent, a rat, a gopher? Why would anyone paint a gopher on a rock as a message? But there it was, painted on a rock. Is it supposed to encourage or tell a story of some kind? Who thinks of painting a gopher? Why? Those were questions that probed my curiosity to research this creature. I was even more uncertain, how was I going to use this as a Biblical reference.

As I pondered this thought I kept thinking of the impossibility of the gopher as an orientation point in the Bible. Would I really be able to place this creature there and make good of its symbolism? It must be there, since we found it. This made me think that there is a suitable symbol for everyone because we are human, we all have different analogies we can relate to and gain inspiration. Nothing escapes our God, or catches Him by surprise, 'nothing' He is not aware of, imagine that!

I must confess, doubt crept in, I wondered, is a gopher even mentioned in the Bible? What would be the reason?

Seemed like I had more questions than answers. I had not even looked in the Bible yet but was already feeling defeated. Is that not like most of us, worried about situations that have not even happened, our thoughts race to the 'what if' and 'worst case' scenarios? We must guard our thoughts so they don't become our ideas and stated words, which the enemy is always lurking around waiting to distract us.

What can I learn about a gopher, and how will I make it interesting? I thought. I could not remember any stories about gophers. I recalled the mention of donkeys, horses, dogs, pigs, lambs, ox, bulls, sheep, goats, even sea creatures, many other creatures, but nothing came to mind about a gopher. Yet the Bible did say, God created all animals, so that would include a gopher, I surmised. I did not even know what a gopher was, so I looked up the meaning, and here is what I found according to Wikipedia, a gopher is rodent *in description.*

"Gophers weigh around 200 g ($\frac{1}{2}$ lb.) and are about 15–20 cm (6–8 in) in body length, with a tail 2.5–5 cm (1–2 in) long. A few species reach weights approaching 1 kg (2.2 lb.). Within any species, the males are larger than the females and can be nearly double their weight.

Average lifespans are one to three years. The maximum lifespan for the pocket gopher is about five years. Some gophers have a lifespan that has been documented as up to seven years in the wild.

Most gophers have brown fur that often closely matches the color of the soil in which they live. Their most characteristic features are their large cheek pouches, from which the word «pocket» in their name derives. These pouches are fur-lined, can be turned inside out, and extend from the side of the mouth well back onto the shoulders. Gophers have small eyes and a short, hairy tail, which they use to feel around tunnels when they walk backward."

A rodent (often described as a negative nuance), has a purpose. What is the purpose of this creation? Although considered an agricultural pest, we can learn a lot from a gopher. Every creation has a purpose. One such benefit, agriculturally speaking, is that a gopher can move enormous amounts of soil every year, and therefore help to aerate the soil. So even with our worst days, we can conclude that we too have a purpose in God's plan; otherwise, we would not be here.

I have often felt like a gopher, asking, what is my purpose in creation? Why am I here to teach others? Would I get it right?

Let us look at it from a spiritual and scriptural reference. God speaking to Noah in *Genesis 6:14 (KJV)* says, *"Make thee an ark of gopher wood; rooms shalt thou make in the ark, and shalt pitch it within and without with pitch."*

This is a specific instruction God gave to Noah in the building of the ark. Gods' protective shield to shelter the chosen few that would repopulate the earth. The ark was a foreshadow of Jesus's position, a one-way path into God's protection from the coming storm upon the Earth. Jesus is our protection, no matter what storm is brewing in our life, he is our one-way path to victory, our shelter from the storm.

While I was thinking strictly as the gopher serving in the capacity of an animal, God use it beyond my understanding. There are multiple uses of what we see and know, it is not always as singular as we often imagine. It is interesting that this is the solution God gave to Noah after telling him the Earth will be destroyed, but he and his family will be saved via this vessel made from the gopher wood. Noah took God at His word and thus began the building of the ark. God most often provides us with more than a single solution to our often-perceived enormous problem. He works with us within our capacity and when we are open, beyond our current knowing.

Up to this point, the Earth had never seen rain; therefore, the inhabitants had a difficult time understanding what Noah was referencing. They laughed at his outlandish foolishness and did not believe him. I wondered, did some of his family members laugh too? We have the Bible to reference and can believe that they took him at this word since his immediate family members entered the ark at the appointed time. But were all his family members immediately on board, and started to help him build the ark? How much convincing did Noah have to do? The Bible does not say.

In my experience of human behavior, I would surmise they too had a difficult time accepting what Noah was making claims to. It took over 100 years for the ark to be finished and God to send the rain, there must have been many that came and went, shaking their heads in disbelief at Noah and his continuous building of this enormous vessel.

But think about it, if it had never rained on Earth before would we have listened and believed that it was from God? *For the Lord God had not caused it to rain, for there was no man to till the ground (Genesis 2:5 KJV).* We can often find ourselves in similar predicament, only limiting our understanding based on current experiences of what we have seen. We hear the phrase, seeing is believing. But is that true, just because we see a thing, does that automatically conclude a belief system? How about all the miracles that Jesus did? Many justified it on account of demonic forces, which asked the question, who did they believe in?

Back to Noah and the lack of rain falling from the sky, the Bible says they had not known rain in that manner until the flood came. *The earth was watered by a mist (from the ground) until the floodwaters came down. There was no mention of rain on the earth until the flood (Genesis 7 KJV).* The Earth and the Garden of Eden were watered by streams, rivers, and mist instead of by rain from the sky (see *Genesis,*

Chapter 2:6 KJV). These sources had been replenished from groundwater. Humidity and mist are still effective today in watering plants. Praise God, the Earth is the Lord's and the fulness thereof.

Back to the gopher. The Bible states *(2 Timothy 3:16 KJV)* *"All scripture is given by inspiration of God, and is profitable for doctrine, for reproof, for correction, for instruction in righteousness."* God's instructions in this case included the very breath of God. Noah had a relationship with God and there was no doubt, he believed he heard God speak those instructions to him, God gave him the exact measurements needed to secure the ark for Noah's family and all the animal occupants. Now, that took an act of faith, see *Hebrews 11* to learn all about the many 'activations' of faith examined from the Bible.

Trusting that God will not lead him into anything less than what was stated, Noah stepped out in faith. The gopher used as a metaphor for the ark represented the energy of God that will surround us. God asked Noah to build the ark of gopher wood that will be further pitched within and without in a layer of protection.

The gopher is defined as a spiritual animal that brings a message of looking, sensing, and being attuned to spiritual and physical attributes that teaches the abilities to listen, feel, and heighten our intuition. It calls us into looking into our growth process and observing where we need to plant seeds, take responsibility for our actions, and not adopting the victim role mentality in blaming others.

The gopher also helps us develop the skill of uncovering hidden truths and meanings and all that lies beneath a situation, which would include our shallow parts. The gopher can survive both above and beneath the ground. A situational model is needed to assess progress and make an adjustment. The lesson is in being able to tune into the guidance of direction when our innate instincts are leading us elsewhere.

In the story of Noah, he was able to tap into this hidden truth and take steps for survival. Noah did not keep his solution hidden it was in plain sight for all to see and partake of. He pleaded for over 100 years, only to have his appeals fall on deaf ears, many choosing to mock him instead. That would have discouraged many of us today, me included. Thank God Noah did not take the easy route to his destination, he believed the word of God for his life and the life of his family. Noah acted on faith, to look beyond his 'now' circumstances to what God promised.

Noah remained focused and I am sure had many days of disappointments and frustrations as he attempted to relay the message of God. Noah trusted in higher knowledge, outside of self, and had a 'go-pher' it (smile) attitude. Noah not only demonstrated consistency in his faith walk but relied on the perfect timing of God.

When we first discovered the gopher painting on a rock, we had no idea what this could mean. God works in mysterious ways, I believe that is one of the reasons He wants us to trust Him, His timing, and His plan for our life. In *Jeremiah 29:11 (NIV)*, God tells us about his specific plan for our life. *"For I know the plans I have for you," declares the LORD, "plans to prosper you and not to harm you, plans to give you hope and a future."*

Observation Point: Perhaps it is a time to dig with a sense of purpose and direction, tap into the resources that you have forgotten because you are more prepared than you realized. Trust in the Lord and lean not on your own understanding as Noah demonstrated.

Our amazing gopher shows us how to maneuver with purpose and keep the balance of instincts in tune with the heartbeat of our purpose. A gopher offers us the wisdom of deeper truths that are awaiting us to pay attention to and then to follow the flow of God's instructions. As we surround ourselves with the complete protection of God's instructions, we will gain the outcome of his promises. As stated in *2 Corinthians 1:20 (KJV): "For all the promises of God in him are yea, and in him Amen, unto the glory of God by us."* When we glory in God, his promises are secured by Him.

Do we have similar experiences today? Jesus said, I am the way, the truth, and the life… How believable is that for the world today? How many are trying to find another solution to life outside of Jesus? Let us faithfully trust God.

Reader's Notes: *Embrace the Message Within*

_____

_____

_____

_____

_____

_____

_____

_____

_____

_____

_____

_____

_____

_____

_____

Chapter 3
A PINK FLAMINGO

W hen I saw the rock painting of a pink flamingo standing on one leg my first impression was of strength. Often when one sees a flamingo, it is standing still on one leg and places the other leg down to walk away. After it reaches its destination, it positions itself back on one leg again proud, and tall.

I became ever curious, why does it stand on one leg? The dictionary states they stand on one leg to preserve energy, a source of warmth and rest. A flamingo can sleep and rest standing on one leg. Oddly, one would think strength comes from standing on two legs to share the weight equally.

Usually where there are two of the same functional parts, if one part is weaker the weight falls on the opposite part. Eventually, that side becomes stronger due to frequent use. There are numerous chapters in the Bible that refer to standing firm, not only in posture but in beliefs, trust, and being planted in the Lord. The Bible refers to standing firm.

Never did it only mention a person's stance. Stand does not simply refer to a posture of feet planted to the ground.

Throughout life's journey there comes a time one should take a firm stand in faith, integrity, love, trust, values, and in their beliefs. Most of us can appreciate a person who stands firm on their word or belief when it is in their favor. Strangely those same people resent when you take the same firm stand of integrity against them. We live in a dual world, and I cannot count the times in my experience when this has happened to me.

I assumed the person who appreciated my integrity would know integrity neither alters nor is a respecter of a person. In all things, do the right thing because it is the right thing to do. *1 Corinthians 15:58 (ESV): "Therefore, my beloved brothers, be steadfast, immovable always abounding in the work of the Lord, knowing that in the Lord your labor is not in vain."*

Growing up, my parents always showed unity and consistency in their actions. My parents repeatedly would say "I don't take up for any wrongdoing." Therefore, we knew they would love us through both good and bad choices. Mind you, the bad choices always came with unpleasant consequences. Eventually, you learn to think before acting on your decisions. I recall one of my siblings would say "mama and daddy never take up for us no matter what". This sibling felt left out because the rest of us did not feel that way. Our parent's response was consistent among all of us. If you are wrong, you are wrong. As a young child, these attributes of integrity and consistency enriched the life that I carried through adulthood. They meant what they said and stood firm.

Our parents modeled this excellent behavior as defined in *Ephesians 6:13 (NIV): "Therefore, put on the full armor of God, so that when the day of evil comes, you may be able to stand your ground, and after you have done everything, to stand."*

How many of us can relate when things do not always go our way? We can choose to see it from our perspective only or consider the other person's point of view. The Bible says a double-minded person is conflicted in all their ways. We need to hold on to our integrity and not compromise depending on who is standing in front of us. God is always present, and we can compromise his representation as believers who chose to be conflicted in our ways.

Standing firm in faith is believing the unseen. In *Hebrew 11:1 (KJV): "Now faith is the substance of things hoped for, the evidence of things unseen."* We hear this chapter of Hebrews being referred to as the 'faith' chapter and it is to an extent of the required steps of those who showed their faith. 'Now' implies that it is believed, whether we see the result, we believe it now. Many of those who the chapter referenced as having enormous faith never personally experienced the 'now' of their faith. That is just it...faith does not need to manifest to be believed.

It is extremely hard and sometimes uncomfortable to stand for what you do not see with your natural eyes. We are a people of seeing is believing. But that is not faith. Most people believe that if you cannot touch it, it is not obtainable, and likely it does not exist. We rely on our five senses: see, touch, hear, smell, and taste to draw conclusions on what one believes to be true. Tapping into the unseen and seeing it manifest goes against our human nature.

Observation Point: Will you be like the flamingo and exercise your strength on the position of your stand? It takes a dedicated effort to stand and be committed to the efforts of your beliefs. Faith takes a 'now' attitude on the promises of things to come. Faith without works is dead, which implies that there needs to be action to activate our faith. Will you be one who stands on the integrity of your faith? Let your faith hold you up as you believe in God.

Reader's Notes: *Embrace the Message Within*

_____

_____

_____

_____

_____

_____

_____

_____

_____

_____

_____

_____

_____

_____

_____

Chapter 4
A RAINBOW

A rainbow is an arch of colors formed in the sky in certain caused by the refraction and dispersion of the sun's light by rain drops or other water droplets in the atmosphere. The pattern of colors starts with red on the outside and changes through orange, yellow, green, blue, indigo, ending with purple on the inside.

The spiritual significance of a rainbow is a symbol of hope, inspiration, promise, and more. Spanning just about every religion and culture, rainbows have been associated with divinity, as a way of transcending the visual representation to spiritual connectivity.

We can leave it as that and move on, not giving too much thought to what it takes to experience a rainbow or the promises that are held within the symbol of the rainbow. What does God say about the rainbow? What is the timing when it is mentioned in the Bible?

Let us look at the significance of when God established this covenant with man. The earth had experienced a flood in which all living things on land perished, including animals and man, except those that were protected with the covering of the Ark, better known as Noah's Ark, made of gopher wood, (see the Chapter on Gopher). After the flood, we see Noah building an altar to the Lord and God promising to never again destroy the earth with a flood and providing a visual reminder of this promise in the sky (a rainbow).

Genesis 8:20-21 (NIV): [20]Then Noah built an altar to the Lord and, taking some of all the clean animals and clean birds, he sacrificed burnt offerings on it. [21]The Lord smelled the pleasing aroma and said in his heart: "Never again will I curse the ground because of humans, even though every inclination of the human heart is evil from childhood. And never again will I destroy all living creatures, as I have done.

Genesis 9:12-15 (NIV): [12]And God said, "This is the sign of the covenant I am making between me and you and every living creature with you, a covenant for all generations to come: [13]I have set my rainbow in the clouds and it will be the sign of the covenant between me and the earth. [14]Whenever I bring clouds over the earth and the rainbow appears in the clouds, [15]I will remember my covenant between me and you and all living creatures of every kind. Never again will the waters become a flood to destroy all life.

The rainbow represents God honoring his words. We are reminded of this in *Isaiah 55:11 (NIV): "So is my word that goes out from my mouth: It will not return to me empty but will accomplish what I desire and achieve the purpose for which I sent it."*

The rainbow represents a sign of a covenant that God has established with mankind. What exactly is a covenant? A covenant is a promise made to humanity by God. It is different from a contract, in that when God makes this covenant, it contains the promises of God to man, despite man's behavior. It is almost one-sided to the benefit of man because man does not have to maintain a position for the covenant to be fulfilled.

It is different from a contract because, with a contract, there are mutual agreements between two (or more) parties where both parties must adhere to their sides of the contract for it to be enforced. With a covenant, despite the outcome from one party, the person making the covenant must maintain the provisions of that established covenant. We see in scripture God established several covenants with man, despite mankind's inability to understand the covenants that would produce success. Mankind often took actions that were self-directed; however, God maintained the covenant he promised on behalf of mankind. In the case of the rainbow, despite man's continual rebellion over the centuries, the covenant was established as a reminder from God to never destroy the earth with a flood.

When I think of a rainbow and all the colors reflected in it, I am reminded of not only the covenant between God and Noah (Noah represented mankind) but also the spiritual significance of the colors, as God often speaks in multiple references from what is in our vision. The seven colors of the rainbow show the completion of that promise from God. Biblically speaking, seven is the number that represents completion. It is the symbol of spiritual perfection. God rested on the seventh-day, having completed all his work in perfection. God even set aside a day to reflect on his creation by sanctifying the seventh-day, calling it holy as unto himself.

There are many examples in the Bible surrounding the number seven. In the book of Revelation, seven is mentioned over 50 times, representing both good and evil. Giving perfect instructions to the church in all matters pertaining to life and godliness, seven epistles were written. Revelations expand upon these epistles to the churches, providing a more in-depth inspired church history.

There are also seven plagues, seven lamps, seven candlesticks, seven angels, seven spirits, seven stars, and seven seals. One could spend valuable time dissecting all the references provided around the number seven, past, present, and future.

There is a remarkable example of the number seven with Elijah and his obedience to God. In *1 Kings 18*, we read about the story of Elijah and his faith in the promises of God. Elijah had prayed it would not rain upon the land until the people acknowledged God. For three and a half years it did not rain in Israel. After a mighty demonstration of the power of God between the prophets of Baal and the God of Elijah, the people started to return to God. Elijah in the wisdom of God knew the timing was now, Elijah prayed for rain.

Even in the knowledge of God's direction, we still need to pray and remain faithful to what God promised. We see this in Elijah's action, his belief, and his dependency on God. Even before he prayed he told King Ahab to go, eat and drink, for there is the sound of the abundance of rain. After King Ahab did as Elijah commanded, Elijah went up to the top of Mount Carmel and there we see him casting himself down to the earth on his knees in prayer for the rain he stated will be coming.

Although God promises to us are yes, he still expects us to pray in reverence to him because our dependency needs to be on God. The heart of man is wicked above all else, we can easily become distracted and take credit for the blessings that God bestow upon us. Elijah had just slew 450 prophets of Baal under the power of God, yet he knew it was not by his might but by the sovereignty of God. Elijah knew his position with the Lord.

This story further illustrates that there is no specific formula on the timing of God. The timing of God is clearly outside the timing of man. Elijah only prayed once when the rain stopped, he only prayed once when God answered his prayer in demonstrating before the people who is the true God. The Bible does not state that Elijah prayed seven times, but taking the liberty, one can surmise that (at least seven times) Elijah prayed to send his servant to observe if there was any sign of rain. The Bible states Elijah sent his servant seven times to view the horizon of the impending rain upon the land, encouraging his servant to look for the rain cloud. When the tiniest cloud began to form upon the horizon, he knew eminent heavy rain was coming and quickly.

I wonder what would have happened if Elijah had become discouraged at the 2nd, 3rd, 4th, 5th, and 6th times; after all, God had answered his prayers at the first request in the past. Our place is to stay in position through prayer, persevering, and believing in the promises of God.

We are living in God's past. God has already done everything we can even think to imagine and He reminds us of this in *Ephesian 3:20 (NIV): "Now unto him that is able to do exceedingly abundantly above all that we can ask or think, according to the power that worketh in us"*. I can imagine Elijah was tempted to give up a little and started to become a little discouraged, but he had a servant to encourage. He kept pressing on for the sake of someone who was depending on him.

Often our plight is not for our sake but for the sake of those who need to be encouraged; those who think God has abandoned them; those who believe there is no God that can love them; those whose life has experienced hurt and pain beyond our comprehension; those who God has placed in our path to shine his light upon; those who often are one step away from believing in Him; those who Satan is constantly reminding of their past mistakes; those who cannot keep wondering why they are in their state of oppression if there is a God; those who are despondent; those who are on the verge of a life-changing decision; those who simply don't know better; those who are looking for another way to fit in; those who need a reminder of a better way; those who simply are discouraged; those who once walked in the light, but is now distracted, etc., the list can go on and on.

So, you might be thinking, how does the story of Elijah link back to the rainbow in our current discussion. Typically, after an abundance of rain what often follows is the promise of God as symbolized with a rainbow. I can clearly visualize Elijah looking up and being assured of the promise with the rainbow in plain sight. It is a covenant that has been made between God and man, that the earth will never again be destroyed with rain (despite the many storms of life). We can hold on to the truth of God's word. Elijah was discouraged right after the grand victory, he temporarily forgot the power of his God. We can relate to Elijah, Satan is never asleep, he comes to kill, steal, and destroy.

Satan was determined to steal the joy of the Lord from the victory the Lord has so faithfully demonstrated to Elijah. Have you been there, one moment you are celebrating the work of the Lord, the next you are questioning, was it really God? I admit it I have been there; we all have. The key is to not stay there too long but find our dependency back on God. Why did God use a rainbow and what does it represent to us now?

The technical formation of a rainbow is described as an arch of colors formed in the sky by the refraction and dispersion of the sun's light by rain and other water droplets in the atmosphere. This scientific definition is remarkably interesting as it defines the very creation of God in Genesis chapter 1, where God was creating, separating heaven and earth in all its formations. Could it be the rainbow was being created at this time as well? We know that God created everything, and nothing was left to chance and assumption.

Yes, I believe that God created the very rainbow that was to be the promised symbol for man because he knew man would need a visual representation of his love for us. There is nothing new under the heaven that has not been made and God has set the discovery in his own time (created for man), so that man will not know everything at once. There is nothing created that has not been created. *Ecclesiastes 3:11 (NIV)* reminds us, *"He has made everything beautiful in its time. He has also set eternity in the human heart; yet no one can fathom what God has done from beginning to end."*

God's timing is perfect and remains perfect for the benefit of man. God lives outside of time; and as a result, can align us to the perfect timing that he has ordained for man to carry out his purpose.

The rainbow is one such symbol of God's timing and revelation for man. Let us dissect each color and expand upon its spiritual meaning as a basic foundational conversation message of God.

The first color **RED** is demonstrated through the redemptive blood of Jesus. The outer layer of anything is its covering, in this case, the atoning blood of Jesus that covers us, our layer of protection. When under the covering of the blood, we are washed and made to look like pure images, by which our Heavenly Father sees us. Look at it this way, a house provides protection from external elements such as heat, cold, or other harmful barriers to the atmosphere. If you are in the house, it will provide a barrier of protection from what is on the other side of the walls of that house.

Likewise, when I think of the external color red forming the rainbow, it reminds me of God's grace at work that protects us from our own unworthy self, due to our sinful nature. But God has provided a means to us all that even the most undeserving sinner, which is all of us, can approach the throne of grace. Despite having sinned and fallen short of the glory of God, the protective blood of Jesus has granted us access to grace to be freely be covered.

The people in Noah's day (God knew) would continue to sin; as we likewise would continue to do, despite the blood of Jesus. God provided the rainbow as a covenant symbol to remind them (and us) that he would cover us with the impending blood of Jesus, the only blood that could cleanse man from his sins. *First John 1:7 (NIV): "But if we walk in the light, as he is in the light, we have fellowship with one another, and the blood of Jesus his Son purifies us from all sin."*

Jesus further demonstrated the importance of the blood cleansing in the great exchange of the last supper with his disciples when Jesus said in *Matthew 26:26-28 (NIV): "While they were eating, Jesus took bread, and when he had given thanks, he broke it and gave it to his disciples, saying, "Take and eat; this is my body." Then he took a cup, and when he had given thanks, he gave it to them, saying, "Drink from it, all of you. This is my blood of the covenant, which is poured out for many for the forgiveness of sins."* Jesus was offering to cover us under his blood; the only blood that can provide that benefit to mankind.

Even Jesus as the Lamb of God had to be covered in his own blood as a provision of our redemption and be presented holy before God, when he took upon himself the sins of mankind.

The redemption and grace of the blood of Jesus are stated in *Ephesians 1:7 (NIV): "In him we have redemption through his blood, the forgiveness of sins, in accordance with the riches of God's grace." Hebrews 9:14 (NIV): "How much more, then, will the blood of Christ, who through the eternal Spirit offered himself unblemished to God, cleanse our consciences from acts that lead to death, so that we may serve the living God!"*

Our covering of the blood (red) of Jesus way back then, represented God's protective covering for our sins and the redemption method of what it would require reconciling us back to our Father. God was providing us the symbol of his covenant promise to man that would further be revealed as man make ready the process of our redemption.

God left nothing to chance, without the shedding of blood, there is no forgiveness of sins, thus redemption. So, the blood of Jesus not only covered us but redeemed us (purchased us back) and now makes provision of grace under its anointing power. Back in Old Testament times, the blood of animals atoned for the sins of Israel, which only covered them yearly. The blood of Jesus redeemed us back, it's not a covering but a purchase, a legal title given back to God. That is a miracle. Hallelujah!

The second color of the rainbow is **ORANGE**, which represents the gift of miracles. We often hear the famous scripture reference that *'I can do all things through Christ who gives me strength' (Philippians 4:13 NIV);* but how many of us genuinely believe that? Truth be told, miracles were really a demonstration for unbelievers. In the New Testament, we saw the crowds continuously following Jesus to have him perform a miracle, even when they had just witnessed one either the same day or the day before...they wanted another one.

A miracle can be described as an act or event which occurs without any scientific explanation, it is likened to the premise of the supernatural. *'A manifestation or event attributed to some force beyond the scientific understanding of the laws of nature',* is how the word supernatural is described according to Merriam-Webster dictionary. As unusual as that is (beyond scientific understanding), human beings have been fascinated with miracles and being on the receiving end of one such phenomenon for centuries. Those experiencing such an encounter often recall the exact place, date, time, and even those that were present during this supernatural event. Memories are as clear and vivid as if the event was currently taking place when retelling the story.

Some of us are like that today, we continue to harp on the miracle of the past as if that is all Jesus can do, a past performance. But let us not be too quick to pass judgments or express a holier than thou attitude. How many of us can honestly say, we do not want a miracle from Jesus to continue to rely on and put our trust in him? Here is where we often miss it. My friends, the wait is over!

Those of us living are experiencing miracles every day. What is that miracle you may ask? The miracle of life, the very breath in our lungs is a miracle. Who can time our breath to the exact science needed to continue life without us even second-guessing this achievement or thinking about it on a continuous basis? Who else has the power to give and take breathe? We might be tempted to say, a doctor can provide breathing via a machine.

Is that indeed the truth of breathing, can it be sustained outside of the external apparatus? What about the quality, would we honestly choose that level of life? God has empowered man with many skills and talents, some of which go beyond our own understanding, especially with inventions and technological advancements; however, let us not get it conflicted with the source behind those giftings and talents.

Often when our limited understanding cannot be defined and measured, we begin to question Jesus and his teachings. We saw many of these examples with the disciples. Men of different genres and professions, each responding to the call of Jesus to 'follow me". On several occasions, each shows the nature of man: doubt, confusion, kindness, good works, selfishness, superiority, self-direction, pride, ego, faithfulness, turning to past behaviors, seeking comfort, including various expressions of love. These were all opportunities to prompt the demonstration of a miracle from Jesus.

I particularly find interesting the story of when the disciples could not cast the demon out of a little boy and the father approached Jesus to express his disappointment that Jesus' disciples could not help his sick son. *Mark 9:14-29 tells* the story of Jesus rebuking the crowd for the lack of faith (along with the disciples), as they all observed what Jesus was saying and doing.

The disciples were puzzled because they had not had the result Jesus demonstrated. They later asked Jesus why were they not able to rebuke the demon from the child? Jesus stated to them that some situations require more than prayer, they will need prayer, faith, and fasting to produce the desired results. We often hear about this three-legged cord that is not easily broken, some situations may take one (pray), another might take two (prayer and faith) and still, others might take all three (prayer, faith, fasting).

Jesus never left his followers in doubt. Even when a miracle has not been demonstrated, we can rely on the words that Jesus shared with Simon (Peter) and his disciples in *Luke 22:31-32 (NIV): "Simon, Simon, Satan has asked to sift all of you as wheat. But I have prayed for you, Simon, that your faith may not fail. And when you have turned back, strengthen your brothers."*

When Satan immediately reminds us of our lack of belief in Jesus, although we profess him to be the answer, we can take comfort in the very words of Jesus. We will go through some trials, but Jesus said he has prayed for us that our faith remains strong, so we can in turn help our brothers. This verse serves as a great reminder that our trials and testing are even more so for the benefit of someone who will need to be uplifted and encouraged along their journey. Miracles are even more for the unbeliever than for believers, our hope is in Jesus.

Sometimes, I think that the 'original' disciples had an advantage in that they had Jesus physically there with them, so it should have been easier for them to constantly believe. But I am reminded of what Jesus said, we will have someone greater than him who will be our comforter, our guide, our conscious.

By providing us the promise of the Holy Spirit to be our advocate, teaching us the ways of God by demonstrating the life of Jesus, we see how Jesus was able to reflect the Father to us. The Holy Spirit is the gift of God the Father, performing miracles for both believers (to be further encouraged) and through believers, their light demonstrates to unbelievers the knowledge and impact of the presence of God.

With Jesus' physical limitation as a man, he could not be in multiple places at once. Remember Jesus was 100 percent man and 100 percent God. The 100 percent man had its natural limitation that did not permit to time-travel from place to place. Although we do read that he had the capabilities to get away from a group immediately without being stoned to death. Jesus knew the way he was to die, and it was not by stoning, but by the way of the cross at the appointed time. As a result, one of Jesus' primary assignments was in healing, both physically and spiritually.

This brings us to the third color of the rainbow YELLOW. Yellow represents healing. Healing often conjures up a physical limitation of the body that needs immediate attention. The need for healing comes in multiple platforms, which include; physical, psychological (emotional/mental), and spiritual. For this writing, we will focus on spiritual healing.

What exactly is spiritual healing? If you google spiritual healing this can take you down a rabbit hole with no escape bottom. There are all types of 'spiritual healing' from mantras attributed to self-love, the seven signs of a deflated spiritual being, the art of spiritual healing of self, signs to check your spiritual health, etc. Again, we will stick to what the word of God provides as wisdom to engage with.

In our fallen state, man has a need to be spiritually healed. We will focus on just three areas of this spiritual healing: Spiritual need, Spiritual source, and Physical death.

1. *Identify The Need for Spiritual Healing*

Ezekiel 1:27 (NIV): I saw that from what appeared to be his waist up he looked like glowing metal, as if full of fire, and that from there down he looked like fire; and brilliant light surrounded him.

The ability to heal stems from the desire to be perfected. We cannot be healed from anything we do not see a deficiency. Spiritual healing comes from a recognition that we are dependent on the enrichment of something outside of ourselves. We are better when we are in alignment with our creator God, the one who knows exactly what we need to be made whole. That comes with an upgraded way of how we see ourselves to a dependent version on the need of our Lord to progress our thinking.

In this passage, Ezekiel's inaugural vision describes as God in all his splendor of the color Amber (gold) awaiting to deliver his healing properties all represented by the dazzling brightness viewed by many spectators. God is waiting on our desire to receive the healing we need to further and amend our path back to him. He is that bright light, in the appearance of fire that will forever surround us.

2. Identify the Source of Spiritual Healing

Ezekiel 1:28 (NIV): Like the appearance of a rainbow in the clouds on a rainy day, so was the radiance around him. This was the appearance of the likeness of the glory of the LORD. When I saw it, I fell facedown, and I heard the voice of one speaking.

Here we see God reminds us of his covenant with man, as the appearance of a rainbow in the clouds on a rainy day. God retells us that He is the source of our healing both internal and external. Who can behold the luminosity of

God, such beauty is beyond compare? God as our source, our Abba Father, who provides the healing we need; our role is to acknowledge the healing source He has provided for our good.

3. *Identify How to Maintain the Spiritual Healing:*
   Dying to Self

Revelation 4:2-3 (KJV): And immediately I was in the spirit: and behold, a throne was set in heaven, and one sat on the throne. And he that sat was to look upon like a jasper and a sardine stone: and there was a rainbow around the throne, in sight like unto an emerald.

Spiritual healing involves death to self. We die to self to embrace the life God has for us. We must realize that only means the things of the flesh is in a constant battle against spiritual enlightenment. The Apostle Paul spoke about this aspect of self in his various letters to the early church. All of which is applicable today in our modern-day church.

In context to the church, we can often view this as the physical building, overlooking the fact that Jesus never said to a building follow me. He always addressed that as of a person because it is an individual choice within the accountability of self to God. We cannot hide behind the building, as believers, our light is to shine, a light can only shine if it is not put out. You must die to self to maintain spiritual healing. When Jesus went to the cross and died in our place (followers of Jesus), we also died at that moment with Jesus. Upon accepting what Jesus did at the cross, we too are healed, have eternal life because of the resurrection of Jesus. While physically here on earth, we are awaiting our expiry of our physical tent (our bodies), into that glorious light, eternal healing.

As with most healings, it cannot be hidden and we want to share it with others, so too is a rainbow, it is in plain view for all to see. The healing properties of the rainbow are for all to see. Life is demonstrated in the breath of the rainbow; it is not hidden. When healing occurs, we see this demonstrated in hopes and dreams of an impending 'new' life. In other words, healing produces newness to life.

The fourth color is **GREEN**, representing intercession and life. The Bible is full of scriptures regarding the necessity of being an intercessor. As believers in Christ, we are all called to be intercessors, one of the primary roles of the believer. *James 5:16 (NIV)* reminds us that '...*the prayer of a righteous person is powerful and effective*'. We see that in *Job 42:8 (NIV)*, God addresses Job's friends this way, '...*My servant Job will pray for you, and I will accept his prayer and not deal with you according to your folly...*'

What is intercession? I would describe intercession as the act of the 'go-between' two objects. As a result of that simple definition, praying as an intercessor means I have the capacity to be discerning in my spirit on behalf of another. Many people call themselves intercessory prayer warriors but without battle wounds or scars to show for the claim. Without intimacy and relationship with God, it is a matter of empty words. We need to be careful who we ask to stand in agreement with our prayer requests.

What spirit are we asking to be invited in our situation? I personally do not want everyone I am acquainted with interceding on my behalf, especially if I am unable to decipher who is representing them. There are a lot of what I call 'word' worship within the body of Christ, those that sound great and have a wonderful orator ability but without power.

True intercessors have an intimate relationship with God. Revelation can be provided to those with a higher ranking in the spirit due to their relationship with God. Jesus is our prime example of an intercessor. The Bible describes Jesus as going out early and spending time with his Father before the dawn of the day. He was constantly interceding on behalf of the people. As a result, he received immediate outcomes when the situations presented itself. We too can learn that valuable lesson, that we ought to always remain in the presence of the Lord, not having to get ready but be ready in any given moment.

We can build that capacity with God through the intentionality of our relationship with Him. One of the greatest, of whom the promise was given, and we are partakers of his righteousness is Abraham. When the cities of Sodom and Gomorrah was intended to be destroyed because of the wickedness of those cities, Abraham approached God as an intercessor for those cities. Here we see Abraham negotiating the terms with God and God agrees with Abraham's proposal. Imagine that God is in negotiation with man. There truly are those with that ability and understanding with God, that they can call upon Him and he will answer, like his friend Abraham was able to do.

What is even more remarkable in this story was the fact that God sought Abraham out to advise him of what was to come. The Bible states that God asked how can he withhold this impending destruction from his friend, Abraham? God had such an intimate fellowship with Abraham that withholding this information from Abraham would have compromised their relationship. God shared with Abraham what was about to happen, and Abraham had the opportunity to negotiate on behalf of the people of Sodom and Gomorrah.

In that final analysis, Abraham depended on his own knowledge, when his final count landed at ten righteous men in those cities, if God would not destroy the cities of Sodom and Gomorrah. Abraham thought surely there must be at least ten good men in that city to spare the cities' destruction. Therefore, he ended his negotiation at ten with God. We know what happened then, God was unable to find even ten righteous persons in those cities to spare their impending doom.

The cities of Sodom and Gomorrah were destroyed with fire and sulfur (or brimstone). God is a just God, and His word will not return unto Him void without achieving the intended purpose. In this instance, there was no promise of a rainbow but a reminder of the justice of God. I believe we can sometimes stop too soon when in prayer as an intercessor on behalf of others. We give up, thinking that it is not the will of God to bring blessings upon that situation. But our role is to keep interceding and let God have the final say. If Abraham had keep going in his negotiating, I believe God would have spared those cities of its pending destruction. But Abraham stopped at ten righteous men, thinking surely there would be ten from those cities. The battle is for the souls of men.

Let us not think we are any better or different than the cities of Sodom and Gomorrah. In our world, there is evil all around, from lying, to stealing, to sexual immorality, drugs, pornography, homosexuality, violence, mind games, etc., we would have an extensive list. While many believe there is a God, they take sin as a joke. They think God will not punish them and have labelled and categorized sin hoping to minimize their sinfulness.

Just as God is quick to accept us when we repent, God does punish unrepentant sinners. God is calling for a people to be set apart, that is what is meant to be holy. The church (the bride of Christ) has often lost its compass. As we blend into the society it is difficult to tell the believer from the non-believer because we do not want to offend anyone and stand out. But that is our very calling, to stand out, to be set apart, to be holy.

The world needs to be able to tell us apart now just like in Jesus' day. We read about Peter who was so like his teacher, Jesus, that when Peter tried to deny Jesus (and he did three times), we were told that Peter was recognized as being a follower of Jesus based on certain criteria, his speech gave him away. *Matthew 26:73 (NIV): "Surely you are one of them; your accent gives you away."*

While on earth, Jesus taught us how to intercede, as he often got away and call upon the Father in preparation for the day's activities. Jesus knew it was not to be his will that he would be responding to, but the will of the Father. He needed to surrender his will to the Father's will. The role of an intercessor was primary to the standard of conduct modeled by Jesus on our behalf. He exemplified intercessory prayer daily, getting away to maintain focus on the intimate relationship with the Father. If Jesus needed to do this, what makes us think we can sustain our walk with God without that necessary time in prayer?

Jesus continues to be the greatest intercessor known to man. Before his ascension to heaven, he made us this promise in *Acts 1:8-9 (NIV)*: *"But you will receive power when the Holy Spirit comes on you; and you will be my witnesses in Jerusalem, and in all Judea and Samaria, and to the ends of the earth." After he said this, he was taken up before their very eyes, and a cloud hid him from their sight.*

Jesus did not leave us alone but provided the promise of the Holy Spirit who would strengthen us to witness to our household (Jerusalem), our neighborhood (Samaria), and the rest of the world (end of the earth). Love starts at home and moves out; we cannot give what we do not have within ourselves. The gift of the intercessor is to provide hope and life to others, just like Jesus modeled on our behalf.

I love the way Jesus stated this in his intercessory prayer in *John 17* (please read the entire chapter to get the complete essence of Jesus' prayer on our behalf). Here are a few verses to get you started:

John 17:9-10; 24-26 (NIV) "I pray for them. I am not praying for the world, but for those you have given me, for they are yours. All I have is yours, and all you have is mine. And glory has come to me through them.

"Father, I want those you have given me to be with me where I am, and to see my glory, the glory you have given me because you loved me before the creation of the world. "Righteous Father, though the world does

not know you, I know you, and they know that you have sent me. I have made you known to them, and will continue to make you known in order that the love you have for me may be in them and that I myself may be in them."

Amazing, hope you love this chapter as much as I do, I can just picture Jesus 'going-in' on our behalf and placing demands (respectfully of course), but due to his ranking was able to lay claims to our success based on his actions (then) and what was to come.

That is what we do when we go into claimant mode with the Father, we remind Him of His words and promises. Our part is to believe and have faith, honoring what the contract (our Bible) states as our duty in God's Kingdom. Again, just simply amazing! Life is modeled with intercession, laying down of ourselves on behalf of another. We are allowed the privilege of standing in the gap for someone else besides our self.

We also see life in a spiritual context as in the multiplication factor when God said to the land (plants/ vegetation), animals, and mankind to reproduce. Without this regeneration, we do not have life. Green represents life in all formats. From the seed placed within the land (plants/ vegetation), the seed placed within the animals to the seed that was placed within mankind, all being created within the six days of God created processes, reflecting on the importance of life within its kind.

It represents our Christian walk, growing and blooming where it is planted. We must be planted in good soil to produce a rich reward. Our Christian growth and experience are being planted in Christ to reproduce good fruits. Living for Christ and finding rest in Him will not only rejuvenate us but will also produce the regeneration needed to do His will. When our life is within the direction of His will, we ultimately find peace in Him, the one that surpasses all understanding. This brings us to sonship and belonging to God.

The fifth color is BLUE, representing knowledge and sonship (belonging). Interesting that when the world uses the word blue it can often represent gloom, depression, anxiety, frustration, unhappiness, like when we say we are 'feeling blue'. Which is a true representation of what the world thinks versus what God demonstrates. If you look up (a positive action), you see a blue sky, representing heaven. Now, how can you feel blue when you are looking up? Seems like an oxymoron to me. Let us break it down, shall we? We all (well most) want to get to heaven, the problem is, we do not want to die to get there, right? There lies the conflict. We must die to transition there, or mustn't we? Ok, ok, get to the point.

We have established that blue represents heaven, which is a reminder of the heavenly realm. The blue that we are seeing is not really heaven but what we see when we look up and most of us think of heaven. There are multiple heavens and what we see is the first level of the sky (which most call heaven). We see this explained in *Exodus 24:20* when Moses (and his sons), including the 70 elders went up to worship God on Mount Sinai:

Exodus 24:10 (KJV): "And they saw the God of Israel: and there was under his feet as it were a paved work of a sapphire stone, and as it were the body of heaven in his clearness."

Sometimes I wish my imagination were grander than it is, so I can pause and elaborate on that envisioned scene. Imagine what they saw as the scripture states, they saw God, and under his feet was a blue layer (a clear blue stone), that you could see right through it, described as the body of heaven. Seems like they were witnessing the atmospheric heaven, the first layer of heaven. The Bible tells us God dwells in the third heaven.

In this context, blue is the color of the spirit that enhances our prayers in terms of our helper, our rescuer, our friend in need. We look up and are reminded of the goodness of God in the heavens.

The knowledge of God for our mind can be contained in the color blue, which represents heaven. The wonder of what that is, is captured in the very beginning of creation, we are told of the creation of the heavens and earth. *Genesis 1:1 (NIV): "In the beginning God created the heavens and the earth."* God is outside of the beginning to be able to create the beginning. God created His dwelling place, nothing can contain God, He is outside of place, time, and space. He all encompasses, a place and Spirit at the same time. Let us pause there for a moment and reflect on the goodness of God on behalf of mankind.

The earth was dark and without separation from the darkness of the waters, that is what it was, a dark watery environment. Then God manifested His glory so we can see it in our limited view with a separation of waters from waters, with what He called a vault. This vault He called sky, the very one we see when we look up. We can appreciate the color of blue to see the work of God for our enjoyment. In this very creation, God was creating for us time and season, as described in Ecclesiastes Chapter 3, which describes the hope of every activity under the heavens. There are no coincidences with God and nothing new that has not been created.

In the building of the tabernacle, several colors were used, one of which was blue in the needlework of the tabernacle curtains. The colors blue, scarlet, and purple were used to make the tabernacle curtains, the priestly garments, the Ephod with the specific details of the breast piece (see

Exodus 36 and *39*). Blue reminded the Israelites of their destination to heaven, representing their divine connection to God Almighty. The Bible does not say this, but it appears blue was always the first color to be itemized in that order, beginning with blue representing spirituality.

As it relates to the knowledge of priesthood, we see Jesus represented all throughout scripture as our great high priest, providing the final sacrifice on our behalf, making us all priests standing before God under the covering of Jesus Christ. Likewise, we have also been brought into sonship with God, because of the finished work of the cross. We are reconnected (reconciled) into our rightful place with God because of the finished work of Jesus. As stated in several verses validating our sonship, we are join-heirs with Christ:

John 8:35 (NIV): "Now a slave has no permanent place in the family, but a son belongs to it forever."

Romans 8:14 (NIV): "For those who are led by the Spirit of God are the children of God."

Romans 1:4 (NIV): "and who through the Spirit of holiness was appointed the Son of God in power[a] by his resurrection from the dead: Jesus Christ our Lord."

I Corinthians 2:12 (NIV): "What we have received is not the spirit of the world, but the Spirit who is from God, so that we may understand what God has freely given us."

1 Corinthians 15:24 (NIV): "Then the end will come, when he hands over the kingdom to God the Father after he has destroyed all dominion, authority and power."

Galatians 3:26 (NIV): "So in Christ Jesus you are all children of God through faith."

Galatians 4:5 (NIV): "to redeem those under the law, that we might receive adoption to sonship."

Ephesians 1:5 (NIV): "He predestined us for the adoption to sonship through Jesus Christ, in accordance with his pleasure and will."

You truly belong to God as His child, having accepted the work that Christ did on your behalf. Be encouraged to seek God regarding any uncertainties. I would encourage you to take the time to understand what exactly happened at the cross. God is the only one that can reassure us of our position in Christ. The Bible says in Ephesian 2:6 (NIV): *"And*

God raised us up with Christ and seated us with him in the heavenly realms in Christ Jesus."

We are now dead in Christ. The question above about dying and going to heaven is just a matter of our earthly body returning to its source, the dust. Death no longer has a sting on us as believers, we belong to God. We have been reconciled to Him. When we accepted Jesus as our Lord and Savior that was the great exchange we entered, the acceptance of his taking our position in exchange with his. The greatest exchange ever known to man, a bargain in my humble opinion.

The fifth color of blue represents grace as five is the Biblical number for Grace. And with that provision of grace, we stand in honor, devotion and are imparted with spiritual wisdom from the blessings of God. What a blessing to fall into that grace, His love of reconciliation.

The sixth color of the rainbow is **INDIGO**, which can be a symbol of honor, devotion, and spiritual wisdom. I call it a transition color from blue to purple (the next color in the rainbow). This in effect represents the continuous levels we can attain when growing; levels of honor, devotion, and spiritual wisdom. Those factors never end and keep us engaged in remembering our dependency on God. We can never give enough honor, show enough devotion, and attain maximum levels of spiritual wisdom without our total dependency on God. The limit of man is exactly that, limited.

Honor without God leads to pride. Most of us have struggled with pride often neglecting the will of God to fulfil our own self-made plans. We rationalize and become wise in our own eyes. The Bible reminds us that pride goes before the fall because one of the brothers to pride is greed.

Scripture reminds us in *James 4:6,10 (NIV): "But He gives us more grace. That is why Scripture says: "God opposes the proud but shows favor to the humble." [10]Humble yourselves before the Lord, and He will lift you up."* If we are not cautious, we will be chasing after the wrong agenda and ending up with this warning from *Proverbs 18:12 (NIV): "Before a downfall the heart is haughty, but humility comes before honor."* We are to be humble, the modesty to refrain from showing our own importance.

Humility is not self-seeking but laying low. This does not mean we are to let others walk over us, by not exercising a backbone, but it does mean not being so quick to toot our own horn that we miss the essence of having someone else honor us before God. Some might be tempted to justify that as being self-confident, but confidence is the ability to feel certain about the truth of something without selling your soul in the process. Having faith in God, outside of self, is the sense of boldness that is dependent on the realization that God is in control, no matter what it looks like in the natural. It is having a conviction that one's destiny is secure in God and humbling self in submission by honoring God with our words and actions.

To be devoted means to profoundly dedicate oneself to a person, cause, or activity. Devotion is the act of consecration in a Biblical context, a sacred observation. It is a transferring of ownership from that of yourself to another. God instructed Moses on how the Israelites were to prepare themselves physically and spiritually to be consecrated before the Lord. They were to be devoted to a cause by following these specific instructions.

Exodus 19:9-12 (NIV): "The LORD said to Moses, 'I am going to come to you in a dense cloud, so that the people will hear me speaking with you and will always put their trust in you...Go to the people and consecrate them today and tomorrow. Have them wash their clothes and be ready by the third day, because on that day the LORD will come down on Mount Sinai in the sight of all the people. Put limits for the people around the mountain and tell them, be careful that you do not go up the mountain or touch the foot of it. Whoever touches the mountain shall surely be put to death.'"

Moses was to prepare the people to meet with God. They were to be consecrated in such a manner to appear before the Lord ready and in a position to receive from God. This was not part of their daily routine but a sacred action of obedience, totally devoted to the instructions of God. Devotion without God leads to self-made righteousness.

We prepare for many things in our life, interviews, new job assignments, various insurances (house, car, life, death, etc.), marriage, where we will live, how we will retire, what we will study in school, what school will we attend, the needs of our children, our spouse's needs, buying a house, buying a car, our own basic needs, even death, all in the hopes of being prepared. The truth is we are not always prepared, many of the events and items we prepare for catch us off guard. We can get caught up with the daily distractions of preparation and miss the mark of preparation and devotion to our Lord and Savior, Jesus Christ.

We need to intentionally put aside daily distractions by spending time in the presence of God and giving Him the reverence He deserves of our time and attention. Our devotion despite the busyness of our daily routine needs to show the importance of God in our life. God calls us to a daily consecration to spend sacred time with Him. A couple of the most important questions we need to be certain of in terms of readiness with God are: How ready are you to die today? Do you know where you will spend eternity?

Wisdom without the Spirit of God leads to worldly wisdom. This is what the Lord says, in *Jeremiah 9:23 (NIV):*

"Let not the wise boast of their wisdom or the strong boast of their strength or the rich boast of their riches". The world is full of wisdom, and most aren't afraid to express their 'wisdom of the ages'.

Since our discussion is more on the Biblical context, we will focus on Biblical wisdom. The Bible has lots to say about wisdom, there are chapters, concepts, and even a book devoted to the topic. If you are fascinated with the topic of wisdom, please read the book of Proverbs. In Chapter 1, the author is identified as Solomon (the wisest man who ever lived), the son of David, King of Israel, verse two states the purpose of the book with its theme is for gaining wisdom and instruction: for understanding words of insight.

The Biblical definition of wisdom is the fear of the Lord. Fear does not mean to be afraid, but to respect and honor God as the source. Therefore, true wisdom is found in obedience to God's principles and standards. As believers, one of the ways we gain wisdom is by studying the word of God. It is a daily source for increasing our understanding of the things of God, which in turn maximizes our spiritual wisdom.

Getting wisdom is loving life and with this love of life, we increase the quality of our life by having a prosperous life. In *Proverbs 19:8 (NIV): "The one who gets wisdom loves life; the one who cherishes understanding will soon prosper."* I do not know about you, but if getting this spiritual wisdom will lead to an increase in my life becoming more prosperous, of course, I am going to love and enjoy my life ever the more.

To clarify, I do not believe this is talking about monetary prosperity (although it would be included) but more of a mindset of true prosperity. We can often look at prosperity as an abundance of financial blessings or increases but having only money does not equate to true wisdom. Statistics tell us of plenty of people who came into great wealth (some overnight) and shortly thereafter were in the exact (or even worst) situation because they did not know how to manage their resources. You can research and find plenty of examples of individuals coming into financial wealth (either via a lottery or inheritance) and within a relatively short period of time, have either wasted it all and are in worst financial situations before they gained the additional money.

The Bible teaches that as a man thinketh so is he. By looking at life through the lenses of God, not just with what is in front of us, we can establish our true possibilities. The mind will start to be renewed to the things of God and not focused merely on the things of the world. As life becomes more concentrated on honoring God, being devoted to His teachings, and being spiritually in tune with the wisdom of God, the color indigo of the rainbow reminds us that we transition and grow with a concentrated effort in the things of God. The things of God take us to a higher plane of kingship and royalty. Let us be reminded our true riches, our heavenly Father, who provides us with everything we need, He has already mapped and planned out our lives, to include all necessary resources, if we choose to follow Him.

The last color of the rainbow is **PURPLE**, representing kingship, royalty, anointing, and the leadership of Jesus. Purple is the symbol of prestige and nobility. To produce the color, (as purple was awfully expensive in ancient times), a combination of two primary colors: red and blue are mixed. As previously elaborated above, red which points to Jesus' blood, His life as a man, and His work on earth, and blue which points to His heavenly dwelling place.

Chapter 31 of the book of Proverbs is often described as the characteristics of a godly spiritual woman which is assessed from how she runs her household to how she conducts business. For our discussion on colors, let's focus on *Proverbs 31:22 (KJV) "She maketh herself coverings of tapestry; Her clothing is silk and purple."* What exactly does that mean?

This woman is a doer, meaning she is making things happen not only for others but for herself. This verse masks itself in the caring of self but let us not stop there. If we stopped there we see this woman only as a mother, wife, and businessperson. We would miss the essence of who she truly is. The *coverings of the tapestry* are a direct correlation to the strength of her ministry. Think about it, the tapestry was one of the items mentioned when Jesus died on the cross as it is being torn in two from the top to the bottom, giving us full access to the Holy of Holies.

The tapestry curtain was a key separation to granting access to the Holy of Holies and only the High Priest was able to get in after atoning for his own sin, then that of the congregation (people of Israel). *Matthew 27:50-51 (NIV): "And when Jesus had cried out again in a loud voice, he gave up his spirit. At that moment the curtain of the temple was torn in two from top to bottom. The earth shook, the rocks split."* This signified our direct 'access granted' to our Father, our reconciliation moment and our ability to approach the throne.

Back to the woman of Proverbs 31, the coverings of the tapestry are of ultimate importance to provide sanctification in its concealment of her secret place with the Lord.

This is followed by an exploration of the next part of that verse; *'her clothing is silk and purple'*. Silk took time to produce and followed a very distinct process to gain the product, mixed with the color of royalty (purple), this woman knew her worth, which was not found in the material things of this world but in the covering of her tapestry. Her worth could be seen by what was wrapping her and how she would use the commodity of the earth (surrounded by uniqueness (silk) and royalty (purple)) to represent and further enhance the provisions of her secret place (her covering).

Yes, it takes time to get to know and have an intimate relationship with God. However, the more we spend time with God, the more we are invited into the secret place and our position is made clear by the very author of our story and the finisher of our faith. When we come into the presence of God, it is only then that we know our true coverings, the tapestry that both covers and uncovers us into the knowledge of true wisdom.

Another Biblical example is Lydia in the book of Acts. We learn about her skills as she conducted business by the selling of purple. The bible simply tells us her name and that she was a seller of purple. *Acts 16:14 (KJV): "And a certain woman named Lydia, a seller of purple, of the city of Thyatira, which worshipped God, heard us: whose heart the Lord opened, that she attended unto the things which were spoken of Paul."*

It is fascinating when the Bible describes an individual by name and profession, it is a direct correlation to their character and how they were known in their respective communities. The Bible says she was a seller of purple. Purple was obtained from shellfish, a highly valuable color that was chiefly worn by princes, and the rich. If she was selling purple, then we can likely presume that Lydia was a woman of means. She was established in the community as a seller of such royal products to receive the title of this profession.

In contrast, we read in *Luke 16:19 (KJV): "There was a certain rich man, which was clothed in purple and fine linen and fared sumptuously every day".* The world can also disguise itself with royalty. But we are not conformed to this world but are transformed by the renewing of our minds when assessing the things of God. While the world will offer us various camouflage of luxury and promises of riches, we need to have the mind of Christ, which can distinguish between the things of the flesh and the spirit-led agenda.

There are indeed riches of the world, all temporal in nature, and all depend on man for its continuation. The riches of God are eternal and do not depend on our works for access. Let us heed this warning; *Revelation 17:4 (KJV):*

"And the woman was arrayed in purple and scarlet colour, and decked with gold and precious stones and pearls, having a golden cup in her hand full of abominations and filthiness of her fornication."

The world provides many enticements. Let us not be deceived, those who have ears choose to hear what the Spirit says in opposition to what the world promises.

If we compare Acts (character of Lydia) to Luke (character of the rich man), we can surmise that the Lord is not against riches but make a distinction on the heart of the person possessing the riches. God wants to provide both types of riches to us but our priority needs to be in alignment with His will and direction. After all, many of our former generals,

Abraham, Isaac, Jacob, and David (to name a few) were rich both materially and spiritually. They knew who the source of their riches was God; and when they called upon Him, they were successful.

In conclusion, we have taken an unveiling look at the colors of the rainbow from a covenant reference to a dissecting of the colors making up the rainbow. What does God say about the rainbow? It is a beautiful reminder of the covenant made with man to never again destroy the earth with a flood. The colors are also significant, and we can extract key principles and messages in our walk with God. May God forever be our guiding principle and source.

Observation Point: God made a covenant with mankind and God will not go against His word. God knows all there is to know about man, providing a way back to Himself through the shedding of Jesus' blood on the cross to reconcile us back to Himself. God has proven that man is not in control of the many signs and wonders exemplified by God, including the rainbow, but man can learn from established covenants. Perhaps we can take God at His word and provide room for Him in the secret place of our hearts so that He can mold us for the purpose we have been created.

The rainbow is a visual sign that calls our attention to God. If we look right now, how many other signs can you see that bring to light the promises of God? How many promises do you know are from God's covenant with man? Many are the hidden promises of God awaiting our discovery to bring us closer to him.

Reader's Notes: *Embrace the Message Within*

Chapter 5
THE CROWN

When we first came upon the image of the crown on the rock, it immediately formed a smile on my face. I started thinking of my impending crown in the next life. Receiving the crown of righteousness (our crown of life) and what it would look like? What did the Bible have to say about the crown? I recalled Jesus coming as a King, but in his first advent he did not even receive an earthly crown of royalty. Instead, he was mocked with a crown of thorns that really pierce into his head. Conflicting images of the crown entered my thoughts.

Who is the King of Glory? The Lord Almighty is He! The crown represents a kingdom, ruled by a King or Queen. In ancient times we saw both Kings and Queens ruling territories to include those with a direct lineage to the earthly throne (descendants of prior kings/queens) or those called to be a king, such as King David from the house of Jesse. King David was anointed to be king of Israel, despite his best friend Jonathan who was next in line to be king, since his father,

King Saul was currently on the throne. When God calls us, we do not need to be qualified in relation to that calling, but God will qualify the called as we see with David.

David was minding his own business, literally doing his chores, tending sheep, when God was instructing the Prophet Samuel to go to the house of Jesse, for that is where he would find and anoint the next king of Israel. In obedience, Samuel went to the house of Jesse in search of the next king.

Now let us not rush to the conclusion that the Prophet Samuel went immediately to carry out this assignment. Samuel had a soft spot for King Saul as he was his prophet. Samuel was used to guiding and providing instructions to Saul from God. This was a difficult assignment for Samuel who mourned for this impending instruction because he knew what it meant to anoint a new king. The Bible tells us that God had to come to Samuel and ask him the following question, *1 Samuel 16:1 (NIV): The LORD said to Samuel, "How long will you mourn for Saul, since I have rejected him as king over Israel? Fill your horn with oil and be on your way; I am sending you to Jesse of Bethlehem. I have chosen one of his sons to be king."*

God sent the Prophet Samuel to the house of Jesse to anoint the next king. When Samuel arrived, he clearly thought the firstborn of Jesse, Eliab would be that person to be anointed, he was tall and good-looking. God said no, keep looking for the one I have called, God does not look at what man looks for but examines the heart of man. Samuel went through the entire sons of Jesse (those that were part of the lineup) only to be told by God, no, that is not the one, keeping looking. When all the sons, that were called by their father to line up to be examined by Samuel, failed to produce the anointed person called by God, Samuel inquired of Jesse, "are these all your sons?"

Then Jesse (*scratching his head – that is my assessment of what is going on now*), suddenly recalled he had another son out in the pasture, tending to the sheep. They must have all been surely thinking that he was not the one called by God. The Prophet Samuel must surely have gotten his assignment wrong, with the wrong household. I could see Jesse reluctantly letting Samuel know he does have another son outside, probably a little embarrassed of the way David would appear from being in the field pasturing the sheep, all dirty and smelly.

But Samuel asked Jesse for that son to be bought in because he was not leaving until he saw David. The story is told that as soon as David came, God immediately told Samuel that he is the one, anoint him to be the next king of Israel. SAY WHAT!!!?

Yes, God is no respecter of persons and will qualify His called. I wonder what was going through the minds of all those present, including David. We can imagine the arrogance and envy of the brothers. We can even empathize with them, if we were in their shoes. After all, David was the youngest son and was to be king over all of them. (*Read 1 Samuel chapter 16 to get a full account of the event.*)

This story also reminds me of the story of Joseph, when God chose him to rescue his family and he would rule over them, they too were not happy and took matters into their own hands. But God will always prevail in his plans.

The crowning of David did not immediately happen even though he has been anointed to be the next king in line to the throne. We do not see David being crowned king until the second book of Samuel. David, while anointed had to learn many lessons and solidify his dependency on God. Many times, God will give us instructions but will not tell us the time, this is to ensure we are continuing our reliance on him and staying in his will and purpose for our life.

2nd Samuel 2:1-4 (NIV) reads, *"In the course of time, David inquired of the LORD. "Shall I go up to one of the towns of Judah?" he asked. The LORD said, "Go up." David asked, "Where shall I go?" "To Hebron," the LORD answered. So David went up there with his two wives, Ahinoam of Jezreel and Abigail, the widow of Nabal of Carmel. David also took the men who were with him, each with his family, and they settled in Hebron and its towns. Then the men of Judah came to Hebron, and there they anointed David king over the tribe of Judah..."*

David had to spend many years in the wilderness for God to prepare him to take over the earthly kingdom in gaining the respect of God's people. It is often in our own wilderness that we come out as God had intended in preparation for our purpose.

I appreciate the way the Bible shows the transition of the kingship from Saul to David in a low-key and neutral manner. Unlike man, God does not need to loudly announce who he has called but you will know them by the fruits they produce. David was such a king, God even called David a man after his own heart. David always sought the advice of God and never forgot it was God who anointed him king, to begin with.

David was a man before his time, in that he praised and worship God with a childlike manner and an abandoned recklessness, it did not matter who was around (including his wife). David acknowledged God in a great way. Now, David was not a perfect human being (none of us are), but he was first to admit his faults before the Lord and knew Him to be the master of his destiny.

The story of David showed the request God directed Samuel to take, but the outcome of that direction depended on both Samuel and David to bring it to fruition. Samuel needed to obey God and David needed to be prepared by God and go through some testing to receive from God. God depends on man to carry out his plans because God has given man authority over the earth. This does not mean God will not use another person if the one he originally called rejects the call. But God's words will not return to him void, having not established the purpose for which it was sent.

The crown represents enlightenment from the Lords' divine goodness. It provided access to authority and power to the kingdom with honor and expected respect from the people. The anointing of David in this instance signified his crowning moment. While David was commissioned to get the golden crown in replacing King Saul, it did not happen right away. But when God sets a thing in motion, we might as well count it done.

The timing of accessing the benefits of being crowned is of importance as well. Let us not be too hasty to finish our assignment, there could be many detours (or look-alike) to the finish line, our directive is to keep looking, just like Samuel had to keep looking until he found the anointed one. One might be tempted to say, how long do I keep looking and when will I know I am at the finish line?

Like Samuel at the very beginning of his calling, he too heard the voice of God but thought it was his mentor and approached him several times. His mentor, the high priest, Eli told him it was not him. Soon enough Eli recognized that it was God and told Samuel how to respond the next time he heard the voice by saying, 'here I am Lord, your servant is listening' (see *I Samuel 3*). We do this by building intimacy with God until we too eventually hear his voice for ourselves.

I do not mean to imply that God will not use others to direct us, but we can and do have the capacity to hear Gods' voice for ourselves.

Another aspect of the crown is what it represents; authority, power, honor, respect, royalty, access, rulership, leadership, and a whole host of parallel descriptive. Let us switch gear a little. In Jesus' coronation ceremony (crowning) he received the resurrected crown of life, likewise, it is promised to us as God's children, because we have been grafted into the family of God.

According to *Encyclopedia Britannica*, the coronation is a ceremony in which a sovereign is inaugurated into office by receiving upon his or her head the crown, which is the chief symbol of regal authority. From earliest historical times a king, queen, or chieftain was inaugurated by some public ceremony; the sovereign might be raised upon a shield, presented with a spear, or invested with a distinctive robe or headdress. In the typical Christian coronation service, the sovereign is anointed with holy oil and receives the crown and other royal insignia from the clergy.

There is an entire formality to the world's coronation ceremony involving the coronation of the British monarch, other European Monarchies' inaugurations, and enthronement ceremonies of various nations. Each represents the culture and traditions from the prior regalia to the next.

According to public information, the coronation of the British monarch is a ceremony in which the monarch of the United Kingdom is formally invested with regalia and crowned at Westminster Abbey. This ceremony takes place several months after the death of the previous monarch, to provide the proper time to mourn, to prepare for the next transition, and celebrate this joyous occasion, the preparation can take months to coordinate.

The ceremony is performed by the Archbishop of Canterbury, the most senior cleric in the Church of England, of which the monarch is the supreme governor. Other clergy and members of the nobility also have roles. Most participants in the ceremony are required to wear ceremonial uniforms or robes and coronets. Many other government officials and guests attend, including representatives of other countries.

The sovereign is first presented to, and acclaimed by, the people. He or she then swears an oath to uphold the law and the Church. Following that, the monarch is anointed with holy oil, invested with regalia, and crowned, before receiving the homage of his or her subjects.

Contrast those views with Jesus' coronation ceremony according to what the Israelites were expecting of an upcoming king, who would rescue them from their current plight from the Roman regime. The current monarchy at the time was the Roman Empire. Since that was Israel's example at the time, they too expected a physical king who would be represented with the perceived royalty of their people, that could then come to rescue Israel from the iron rule of Rome. Jesus did not represent the image they had in mind, in terms of royalty; after all, many had grown up with him and knew him as a child.

It can be understood from the logical expectation of the people in Israel who were awaiting their king and expecting a grand ceremony that what Jesus was offering was not very appealing. There was no fanfare in Jesus' announcement that he was 'the king' they were waiting for and to follow him. Here was a man they had grown up with (for the most part), they knew his parents, his siblings, other relatives, and he was proclaiming himself the expected king of ancient days. How could that be? That question has not gone away even to this day, man is still attempting to put logic to the plan of God.

Let us examine what Jesus' coronation ceremony accomplished for man in which ultimately man will receive the crown of life.

James 1:12 (NIV): "Blessed is the one who perseveres under trial because, having stood the test, that person will receive the crown of life that the Lord has promised to those who love him." The greatest crown man can receive is the crown of life because we hold to the belief of the promise of the Lord, Jesus Christ, of our eternal life.

Imagine that the greatest victory of our actual crowning comes in the afterlife, where each of us will receive the crown of life. However, the promise does not begin in the afterlife but starts with our life here on earth. The Bible says that we are blessed when we persevere under trial and have passed our test, that we will receive the crown of life. Often, we misunderstand our testing in this life as to interpret that God is not on our side, that somehow, we have failed and are unable to determine what we have done wrong. We start to blame others, our environment, our circumstances, even ourselves in the justification and understanding of what we did that we did not live up to Christ's expectations.

We have evidence in the Bible that tells us we will go through trials; however, our position is to continue pressing through believing that Christ is our foundation. I used to think that to persevere means to endure something but I realized it is more than that. Yes, it means to endure something, but it also means to keep going even if there is little to no prospect of success. When I evaluate my spiritual walk with Christ, he is saying those exact words to me, "keep enduring even if there's little to no evidence a prospect of success in this life. You will receive a promised crown of life if you do not give up and stood the test of time."

I think the Apostle Paul demonstrated that concept best as a model of this expectation from Christ. Paul was commissioned to preach the gospel, the good news. In his many voyages and many unknowns, including his numerous imprisonments and those who chose to do him mental and physical harm, Paul passed the test of his trials and persevered in his calling. He kept the faith; he finished his race. As with a victor's crown in the natural, we have an anticipated victor's crown when we too have finished our spiritual race on earth. The crowning we receive will be demonstrated by the righteousness of the faith we employ on earth.

May I pause here to encourage you today in your faith and to please endure to the end; after all, we are only here for a brief period to run our race as assigned by God. He has promised to never leave us nor forsake us even in that testing period of our assignment.

Observation Point: As in the natural, the crown represents authority and power to those more privilege than the common person. Those with a right to rule and exercise influence over the common public. There is authority and power that comes with this crown, the less privileged must follow the directives from those in control. This is how it is done in the natural, on earth. The reality of the crown on earth is that it is interchangeable.

Picking up that rock that day made me observe that human dynasties are just that, humans. When one dynasty is extinct, it is easily replaced with a successor, we have seen many exchanges of earthly kingdoms even in Old and New Testaments times. The only everlasting dynasty is the one held under the provisions of Almighty God.

We know the visible operates differently from the invisible. While we are living on earth, we know that our greatest reward is established in the afterlife, the eternal world to come. This is where we will receive our true crowning, the imagination of man is too limited to think of the details of such a much-anticipated event in glory. How about you, will you be ready to be crowned? Have you imagined what your crown will look like?

Reader's Notes: *Embrace the Message Within*

Chapter 6
PANDA BEAR

It's not every day that you stumble across a brightly-colored rock with a panda on it! I had to examine it because, of course, this was an intentional placement. The artist wanted me to appreciate their craftsmanship and time. A rock with an animal may be common, but what stood out the most was this animal was a panda! A panda isn't your average day animal. This was intriguing. This brought many questions to mind. Is a panda their favorite animal? Do their kids like pandas? I needed to make sense of this intentional treasure left for me to find. I am not writing to assume anything about this painted rock, but I do want to share what I found out about the panda that fascinated me, and maybe it will be as thought-provoking for you as well.

To be honest, as I was researching information about the panda bear and the only time that a panda bear comes to my mind is when I'm at the zoo with my children or grandchild. Panda bears are known for black patches around their eyes, over the ears, and across their round bodies that serve to camouflage. The white body helps to hide in the snow and black markings help to retain heat in cold environments. The color pattern on the panda's face is used to communicate with other pandas.

Pandas are large black and white mammals native to South Central China. They are classified with bears. They are called giant pandas to distinguish them from the red panda which is found in small, isolated mountain regions about 4,000 feet high in China, Nepal, India, Bhutan, and Burma. Even though giant pandas affiliate to and are structurally created to be carnivores, they truly are "folivore", which really means an herbivore that specializes in eating leaves. They primarily consume around 99% of bamboo shoots in their diet. The amount of bamboo is hard to digest and has very little nutritional value. Pandas eat about half their weight in food each day. Panda bears can eat up to 14 pounds of bamboo daily. A giant panda can consume 28 pounds of bamboo daily. An adult panda can consume 40 to 80 pounds of food daily. The one percent consummation is shrubs, roots, vines, and weeds.

The fact that a panda bear eats something that brings little to no nutritional value made me think of my own life. This had me thinking, why would the panda bear or anyone else consume anything that supplies little or no nutritional nourishment to their body? This problem doesn't only apply to the four-leg animals but humans as well. The conditions and demographics play a major part in people's overall health. I know we expect people from undeveloped countries to experience poor eating habits due to the shortage of food supply or limitations on what the ground can produce. They too need a nutritious daily diet to survive without any health complications. Let's bring this closer to home, America.

As hard as it may be to believe, even America has people going to bed hungry and sick due to the lack of nutritious food. The modern society feeds on unhealthy fast food. We want everything fast. We live in an instant society. If we can't get it fast, is it even worth it? There is much more to learn from the giant panda. Stick with me, because I want you to grasp where I am going with all that I found.

I found it strange that an animal that was created to eat meat and other plants would divert to eating bamboo. The species of panda bears that once had meat and more nutritional food to survive on in their environment chose to be restrained to an area where only bamboo grows. Think about it. This species that could have wandered freely in the forest, allowed their choice of food to end up bringing them into isolation. Isolation to the point of extinction. Today they are considered vulnerable species.

Like many people, the consequences of former generations' bad choices or lack of put them in a position for man to take notice of their need for food; which handicapped the pandas. This put them in a place to depend on men to survive to prevent extinction. Wow! How many times have we believed that others had our best interest and it turned out to be a cage of unlived dreams? The times that you and I thought we had to depend on someone else's "approval" or keeping up with the Joneses; only to find out that we were free all along and didn't need anyone but ourselves.

Pandas are not very sociable because they are too busy consuming food to interact with other pandas, even their own cubs. Consumption is their top priority. I can certainly see where people share that same action. We get too focused on chasing a dream, money, goal, or in our phones that we become absent from being present with our family and friends. Then, before we can realize or recognize it; depression or envy has crept into our hearts. We become so worried about what others are doing, scrolling to see how everyone is showing up on social media, that we are consuming the negativity of what is going on in the world and not feeding ourselves with a healthy lifestyle of being.

The more I thought about it the more I realized how we humans can relate to the panda bears in many ways. The good or not so good choices we make in life. These choices are not always the best for us at the present and can be passed onto our next generation. Many people don't realize the importance of our upbringing and what is passed down to us. Different nationality has their own way of eating and preparing food. Like the panda, we rely on what's around us to survive. Some parents are just concerned about putting food on the table and not too concerned about the nutritional value it gives to sustain the family. I believe every choice we make or don't make affects somebody either directly or indirectly.

The Bible tells us that at the beginning of creation, Adam and Eve lived a life of plenty and God walked with them. Yet, their choice to change the narrative affected them and how we live today. Yes, their "sinful" nature, of not listening to God, was passed down to us. Thank God He sent His son Jesus to redeem us from sin. Don't ever think we can do anything or live any way without any repercussions from our actions. No one gets a free pass. Many may think or look as though someone has gotten away with it. Not true! They may not reap the aftermath of bad decisions right away, but it will come. Most of the time it will come when one least expected. Have you ever heard "it rains on the just and unjust?" Yes, both will get wet! I have lived long enough to realize bad choices will take you farther than you want to go and cost more than anyone wants to pay.

Like the panda bear, making a choice against our true nature will always lead to destruction. But the beautiful thing about the symbolism of the panda is it represents balance, harmony, peace, gratitude, order, territory, discretion, gentleness, nurturing emotions, determination, and personal boundaries.

As we learned the panda vastly rely on bamboo as their source of food to survive. Therefore, they are territorial and enjoy their personal boundaries. Does that sound familiar? I believe it is important to set personal boundaries to ensure a healthier and balanced life for yourself. You need to know what you will not tolerate in your life. The boundaries that you set for yourself need to be firm and well established that no one will knowingly cross them. If someone or something questions or gets offended by your personal boundaries that's a form of disrespect. You are worthy of all respect.

The panda moves slowly to reserve its energy. We can learn from this. We need to take this concept of being conscious to slow down our pace in life. We live in a generation of "fast," "instant," "hurry up and wait." If you are like me, I love lists. I love making and completing everything that I put on my list and my husband's 'honey-do' list. But I am realizing that like most of us we rush trying to get things done just to wake up and do it all over again. Honestly, we never check things off our list because tomorrow brings another list. That makes no sense, we come slave and dependent on 'a list'.

We read in *Matthew 6:34 (NIV): "Therefore do not worry about tomorrow, for tomorrow will worry about itself. Each day has enough trouble of its own."* This tells me that sometimes we rush into things that later we live to regret. Some may say God is taking too long and rush into things and then blame Him for not responding on their time schedule. God gives us enough strength we need for the day and all that comes with it. Often it may be hard to believe that there are some areas of our lives we need to trust and condition ourselves to have the patience to work and move more effectively. God has His own timing. He knows things we don't know and sees what we don't see. Therefore, to prevent unnecessary pain, overexertion of energy, and disappointments, just be "still." No one can think effectively when the mind and body are tired.

Just as the panda is adaptable, I feel we as humans adapt or adjust to the same routine in life. Many go to work, come home to family, eat, sleep, and get up and do it all over again. Many wait until retirement day only to find out you no longer have the desire, the finances or feel up to doing all the things you put off. Yes, like the panda who learned how to adapt to its environment and circumstances that were laid out for them. We as people can take it many steps further. We have the choice to choose our directions. Either to survive and accept whatever life hands us down or strive with what life hands us down.

We no longer need to just survive but to strive toward goals in life. There are circumstances and life's challenges that may seem unbearable to handle. In some portion of our lives, we will all experience them. There is no way around or getting out of it. In *Isaiah 54:10 (ESV): "For the mountains may depart and the hills be removed, but my steadfast love shall not depart from you, and my covenant of peace shall not be removed, says the Lord, who has compassion on you."*

The mountains and hills refer to disappointments, grief, trouble, loss, and problems in life. Now it will be up to every individual to learn and grow from their experience. If not more than likely when it comes again, a repeat of the same outcome. Be wise, learn, and become better, not bitter. Adapt to what brings you strength through the process and lean in to ride the waves of life and land on both feet.

When it comes down to it, it's all about taking proper care of our Mind, Body, and Soul. We have heard it said, the mind is a terrible thing to waste. Yes, we can waste our mind polluting it with negative thoughts we tell ourselves, evil actions, and not living to our fullest potential, which impacts our destiny.

The body can be compromised by not fueling it with healthy choices, unnecessary stress and anxiety from life, and addictions. We probably have heard getting at least 6 to 8 hours of rest, which is important. Sleep restores and renews our bodies.

The soul is the center and essence of who we are. It needs special and proper balance that only we can give it by prayer, meditations, affirmations, taking time for ourselves through self-care, and loving ourselves.

Observation Point: My dad used to say that we should learn at least one thing every day. Today, as I am writing this, I have learned many things that inspired me from the lives of the panda bear. To be mindful of how passing generational actions are not always beneficial in the present generation in living the life we are destined to live in fullness and plenty. By learning from other's past mistakes, lessons, and even dependency we should be open to adapt our ways to ensure that our present and next generation have a better life.

Reader's Notes: *Embrace the Message Within*

_____

_____

_____

_____

_____

_____

_____

_____

_____

_____

_____

_____

_____

_____

Chapter 7
VOTE – A CENSUS

We had an upcoming election and one of the rocks we found simply stated 'Vote'. I thought this was interesting. While as inspirational as the previous rocks, the message was profound. We were called to vote and exercise our rights to that process, so many before us had fought to provide the upcoming generation a voice.

The act of voting (or taking a census) is to promote placement to a position and or location and can represent being honored or dishonored. Again, we will look at this from a Biblical perspective. In the Bible, we saw various ways people or groups were voted into or out of position and the consequences of that action.

One of those dishonoring incidents was recorded in *1 Chronicles 21* when King David, outside of the will of God, took it upon himself to count the fighting men of Israel because they defeated the Philistines. David started to be self-reflective, self-reliant, and self-dependency as he executed his plan to count the fighting men in his army to show his physical strength and presence. Notice the keyword here 'self'.

David had experienced numerous victories in the battles over the Philistines at Gezer and he was starting to 'feel himself.' As a result, David commanded his lead officer Joab to take a census of his fighting army. His right-hand man, Joab, questioned David's outlook on this, but David disregarded his inquiry. Joab followed King David's request to take a census of Israel's army.

I believe this happened because God was testing David's total loyalty in believing that God was indeed fighting for the Israelites and not the dependency on the amount of David's physical army. I believe so because the next chapter states that Satan incited David. Satan is always waiting for an opportunity to entice us out of the will of God. Satan is always on assignment, he is very patient and if he doesn't get us one time, he comes back at an opportune moment, often when we have forgotten about him. Satan must get permission to inflict any misappropriation with a servant of God. At times it is our necessary test.

Another example of this, we see in the story of Job (see the entire story of Job in the book of Job).

In chapter 21 of 1 Chronicles, it said that Satan incited David, which meant that God gave Satan permission to test David and his true dependency on God. Unfortunately, David failed the test. Even when he was given counsel against taking this type of action from his lead officer, Joab, David still did what his flesh wanted to do. That of showing the battle was in part due to their own ability and not fully reliant on God.

Now let us not be too hasty to pass judgment on David, because we are reading the story and can see both the beginning and end of the situation. David was not outside of the will of God when he failed this test. While we can be in the will of God, we must recognize that Satan is always there as well asking for permission to lead us astray. We must be on our guard to overcome the desires of the flesh and do things our way. The Bible stated that Satan incited David, which means he was there during David's victory over his enemy. Satan saw this as his opportune time to lead David astray from God's provisional protection.

In retrospect, would we have passed the test? I wonder how many times God has showed up in my situation and provided the outcome he has promised, and I turned around and never acknowledged him. While it is true that the human factor was involved in that they physically fought against the Philistine, David forgot that it was God who delivered the victory.

As humans, we have two natures that are in constant battle; the flesh and the spiritual. Since the world appeals to the flesh, man is prone to take orders from the flesh, often overlooking our spiritual nature. We forget that the one we feed more often is the dominant one.

In this battle, with David feeding his fleshly desires, we can still appreciate the mercy shown by God. Because God is both appropriate and merciful, David experiences the justice and love of God. We, too, do not escape the correction. When we knowingly choose to disobey God's voice he will present consequences to correct our course. In David's case, the direction he was warned against but chose to overlook. The Bible tells us that God reminded David of who was in control. God presented David with three choices of how he would like to be punished for his disobedience.

Let us think about that for a moment. Imagine God coming to us to ask how we would like to be punished for willful disobedience and we get to choose our punishment. I wonder how many would say, 'but God...why do I need to be punished?' We must remember that God cannot turn a blind eye to disobedience, he must deliver justice. God is both love and justice.

God could have simply just wiped David off the face of the earth, not provided another opportunity for David to repent (after all, he had already warned him), and simply let it be David's consequence. But God! Not only was God able to do this, because he is a God of his word, but he has also promised David certain provisions and he simply could not go against His own words. But God is also a just God and will punish us for our iniquities.

God gives us a choice every day, to follow him or continue to do our own thing. God says he has a plan for each of us, a plan to give us a hopeful future and not to harm us. Most of us do not take God at His word, we continue to do our own thing. And as we have experienced, the law of cause and effect applies in the spiritual just as is in the physical. Another way to look at this, is that God loves us too much to leave us in our own created messes. He always has a way out for us if we so chose to take the options provided to us.

Again, let us not judge David too harshly, the Bible states David was a man after God's heart. David had a repentant heart, a heart of change, a heart of the redo, a heart that wanted to ultimately please God. David chose to appeal to the mercy of God and asked for God's justice to be done quickly, he did not want to leave his future in the hands of man. Smart man! We have so much bias than God can ever be. God continues to show mercy, grace, and love despite man's choices.

God allowed David to have his choice by sending a plague over Israel, this resulted in the death of seventy thousand men, and when God saw David's repentant heart, the Lord stopped the angel of death. Imagine that God relented when man changed his heart. The Bible does not give us the specific timeframe when the angel of death was in action, but I would say it did not take much time for this to happen since this was to be a three-day punishment.

This shows the mercy of God towards men, sending his son Jesus to protect us from the enemy of death and providing for our victory. Jesus paid the only payment that could be accepted to stop dead in its tracks by taking away our sins and giving us the opportunity to repent and accept his salvation covering.

The death that we chose, like David, we had no clue to the lasting meaning of that choice and God stepped in and save us by offering his Son for our redemption. Jesus paid the price in full to stop the angel of death, in three days it would have been all over for Israel, but God relented and provided a way out. Just like in three days, Jesus overcame the powers of death by stopping that power given to Satan and providing the option to us with eternal life.

We are no different when it comes to the mercy of God. O' the mercy of God! While the angel of death was in action, God saw how sorry David was and how he called upon the mercy of God and as a result, God called off the angel of death to stop. David appealed to God to take his life instead since it was his decision to take the census against of the will of God. God accepted David's plea (by halting the death angel's action) and built an altar of burnt offering to God in the place where death had stopped as a memorial of the goodness of God.

Let us learn from this response as God continues to show his faithfulness to man. The Psalmist asks, "Who is man that God is mindful of him?" God has created man for a purpose on the earth, may we continue to seek his purpose for our creation and always be in alliance to his will for our life. May we too build an altar of offering in gratitude of the provisions from God.

May we, like David, learn this valuable lesson of acknowledging God as our provider and follow His lead. David was not perfect in his walk with God, none of us are, but a great takeaway from the life of David is his ability to recognize his limitations, truly repent, and seek the newness of God.

In the provisions of his offering, David could have offered a burnt offering to God that did not cost him anything in return. In fact, David was offered freely the animals to be sacrificed to God as a burnt offering, but David paid the owner full price for the animals necessary to honor God because of his disobedience. Once more another test for David; would he sacrifice to the Lord something that did not cost him anything as a sacrifice of obedience? A truly repentant heart will always pass the test of obedience.

It is not to say, we will not be tested, but will we pass the test? It will cost us our fleshly desires to be in obedience to the true sacrifice of our offerings unto God. A valuable lesson to advance us to the next level in our obedience of growth. The Lord responded to David by answering him with fire upon the burnt offering of his sacrifice. The Lord will always meet us at the level of our heart's response. He will never impose himself in our heart.

We see this in the beautiful promise of Jesus in *John 15:16 (NIV): "You did not choose me, but I chose you and appointed you so that you might go and bear fruit, fruit that will last and so that whatever you ask in my name the Father will give you."* We were voted in with the selection of the Father by appointing Jesus to die for us to reconcile himself to us. This rock served to remind me of God's choice in choosing me, he voted for me as his child.

The way of the cross is our exercising, our voting privilege to belong to the family of God. Making the provision for us to be reunited with our heavenly Father, did not devoid us of the earthly right to make our choice. Jesus wants all of us to come to him, but it is not a forced decision. In *Matthew 11:28 (NIV): "Jesus said we should come to him all who are weary and heavy laden, and he will give us rest."*

I do not know about you, but I take comfort in that promise, it does not state any other provision but to come and he will do the rest. We must take the first step; come, which is to overcome our hesitancy, and he will do what is necessary to give us rest. Our action is predicated upon his action towards us.

When we cast our vote, who's approval are we seeking? *Galatians 1:10 (NIV): "Am I now trying to win the approval of human beings, or of God? Or am I trying to please people? If I were still trying to please people, I would not be a servant of Christ."* This is such a powerful perspective when it comes to human beings. We are usually trying to win the approval of man and not of God. This is often demonstrated in our actions and emotions.

I can certainly relate to my flesh when I am trying to please others, I tend to get very frustrated and can be quickly irritated. When I redirect my thinking to that of the expectation of God, I find myself not so easily distracted by the natural demands of others. The litmus test is to ask the question of whose approval I am trying to win.

In the example above, David may have been seeking the approval of man, although he already had the approval of God. He was already assured of the victory without having to count the number of men in his army. There are times God will give us the direction to count the number who is on our side, or the number of men needed to secure the instructions of God but let us not be too swift to assign those instructions as always God led.

Contrary to David, let us look at the story of Gideon. God described Gideon as a mighty warrior and Gideon did a double take as to who God was speaking of, surely not him.

We read the story of Gideon in chapter six from the book of Judges. Gideon was called upon to save the Israelites from the Midianites by going into battle. Gideon was like, "say what? Surely you are not talking to me? Gideon presented legitimate arguments to God and reminded God of who he is and what tribe he belonged to, giving God all the reasons, it was not him being addressed by God. Yet God's reply was, Yes to all of that; but here is what I want you to do, get an army together and I will give you the victory. (Some paraphrasing here).

Gideon still was not convinced and called upon his brother's tribes to help him prepare for battle. He assembled thousands upon thousands of willing men to take on this task. God was not having any of it and told Gideon to reduce the number of men he had to fight in the battle against the Midianites. Again, I could see Gideon saying, "'say what?' God, you asked me to go into battle and now you want me to reduce the number of helpers I have for this impossible task, I do not understand. Surely this cannot be directly from God."

In this situation, God was positioning Gideon to trust him and know that the battle was already won, but Gideon needed to be obedient and depend on God's instructions. Gideon, in God's fashion, was chosen by God, so that God's glory can be revealed. Here were some of Gideon's justifiable case references in his defense:

(1) Gideon stated his clan was the weakest in Manasseh

(2) He was the least in his immediate family

(3) God had not provided them victory as he promised their ancestors

(4) God has given them over to the hands of their oppressors, the Midian.

All valid concerns, but God simply replied to Gideon, "Go in the strength you have because I am the one sending you to save Israel out of the hands of the Midianites."

Imagine God saying that to us when we are feeling the exact sentiments that Gideon presented to God. God, I am not good enough; who am I to think I can do this thing that you have called me to; I know you did it for someone else and saw their victory; but where are you in this time of my life, how can I be sure it is you, God? Show me a sign, please Lord!

God showed up for Gideon and he is the same God that does not change. God understands our conflict and questions of his abilities, but he still wants us to trust him. The battle belongs to him, and he wants us to stand still and know that he is God. God chose Gideon for such a time as this to prove to the children of Israel that he had not forgotten them, but they needed to trust him. God chose him to lead the battle with the tribe that they had considered the least so that his glory can be seen. God was the one who chose Gideon, he certainly did not choose himself, having already justified the reasons he could not be used by God.

Gideon was still unsure and wanted God to prove that He was the one speaking with him and not his imagination. Gideon asked God to prove Himself at least three times that it was the Lord speaking with him. God is so merciful and indulged in Gideon's requests.

Gideon's first request was for God not to leave him until he has prepared a food offering. God honored this request. Gideon felt a little better but was not totally convinced, the next request was for God to show his presence by the demonstration of using a fleece that Gideon asked to remain wet overnight when everything else around it was to be dry. When this happened, Gideon was like, "Well can you do the opposite Lord, let everything but the fleece dry and everything else around it be wet?" The Lord obliged Gideon's request as well. God granted all three requests from Gideon as proof that God was indeed directing him to lead the battle against the Midianites.

Gideon was still scared because by this time word had gotten out and now the Midianites had help from other countries...the Amalekites and other Eastern countries have joined forces against Gideon. In true human form, what did Gideon naturally do, he too asked other countries to join him in the battle, he sent messengers from his tribe (Manasseh) to seek help from their 'brother' tribes of Asher, Zebulun, and Naphtali for help.

But God was not in this request. God told Gideon he had too many men to fight against the Midianites because God was not going to deliver Midian into Gideon's hands under this circumstance. Since it would be their own hands to provide the victory and not God, there would be no credibility from the hands of God that he had indeed provided the victory. Gideon had a dilemma. Gideon had to make a choice, would he listen to his natural flesh or take instructions from God? Gideon, being a God-fearing man, listened to the voice and instructions from God, he obeyed.

I pause here to reflect on what it took for Gideon to obey and not provide excuses. Would I be that quick to obey? Would you?

Gideon was instructed to reduce his forces from thirty thousand capable men down to a mere 300. Prior to this Gideon was already a hated man, since he had destroyed the altar of Baal, the foreign god, and the Midianites were furious at him for this action. Gideon was really beginning to live up to the title that God has granted him, 'mighty warrior'. Can it be when God has given us a title, we can truly live up to that name, as described by God upon us? There are so many examples of this in the Bible, Abraham, Jacob, Gideon, Deborah, Samson, Naomi, Mary, John-the Baptizer,

Peter, Paul, just to name a few. Who has God called you to be and what is your reference point of acceptance?

Gideon had let his past and present circumstances defined who he was but when God intervened and showed him who he truly was, Gideon lived up to his position in God. That did not mean, Gideon did not endure self-doubt, the ridicule of others (especially his enemies), but he acted despite those oppositions. Here we saw the numbering of the people was for the glory of God, which demonstrates that any God given situation, can be used to illustrate the purposes of God. When we are willing to be his vessels for the greater good, there is resolution in our pain.

Most of the decay of the situational plights that the children of Israel found themselves in were when they chose not to acknowledge their promise to God, that is to put him as their only God and follow his instructions.

Observation Point: We can often be asked to cast our voice in voting or taking a census that dictates our position. This comes in a variety of ways, where we live, where we work, who we associate or not associate with, our formal and informal beliefs, businesses we support, people we support, agendas we support, the list can go on forever. We all have an opinion, a position that references who we are, how we want others to view us, how loyal we are to a cause, how true we are to ourselves or those who are important to us.

Could it be that we are not so different today from the children of Israel who wandered in the desert? Making promises we are unable to keep, seeking forgiveness only to repeat the same offense? How different would it be if we knew the outcome of our destiny, would we make different choices? We do know, just like the children of Israel knew the consequences of their actions, that when we enter covenant there are cause and effect with God. We, too, know the consequences of making actions against His will as well as according to His will. Yet, we make those choices; in essence we cast our vote.

God's final census will be the ultimate vote, the Bible tells us that he is keeping a book of life with the names of those who are His. Will you be counted amongst God's finalists? Be sure to secure your spot. If you are not sure, this symbolic prayer will secure that result when repeated from the heart.

Lord Jesus, thank you for dying on the cross for my sins. I confess I am a sinner and need cleansing. I accept the gift of salvation and ask you to come into my heart and help me to live the rest of my life for you. In Jesus name I pray, Amen.

Friend, it is as simple as that, if you confess the Lord Jesus with your mouth and heart you are saved. The Holy Spirit will be your teacher on how to live a faithful life. Welcome to the family of God.

Reader's Notes: *Embrace the Message Within*

_____

_____

_____

_____

_____

_____

_____

_____

_____

_____

_____

_____

_____

_____

Chapter 8
CAMEL

This was no ordinary day. I had set out to take a walk around the block of my church and in true 'Joshua' format, walked around the building seven times to tear down any walls preventing victory towards all who entered the church doors. There I was, walking around the building, and not sure on what count, when I saw painted rocks with a pack of Camel cigarette laying besides the painted rocks. While not typical, my mind immediately went to the 'other' painted rocks and I said to myself, why not? God can indeed speak in any manner and fashion he so choses. I took a picture of the rocks, the cigarette carton an all and thought, "Yes, this can be a subject in our upcoming book, the camel."

In understanding some of the camel's implications in the Biblical context, let us dissect the camel for an appreciative reference. There are primarily two types of camels, the dromedary (one hump) and Bactrian (two humps), from which stems a variation of the camel family, like the South American llama, alpaca, vicuna, and guanaco. The Bactrian is native to Asia (China and Mongolia) while the dromedary camel exists primarily in the native land of the Middle East and Africa. With that being the case, since the location of the Bible is mainly the Middle East, we will assume the dromedary type were the ones referenced in the Biblical context.

What is in the camels' hump, you asked? Great question! Most of us assume the camel's hump is where water is stored, in preparation for hydration during times in the desert, but that is not the case, the hump is the actual storage of fat. Although a typical camel can drink up to 40 gallons of water in a matter of minutes (keep this information handy as we explore the implication of this amazing fact later). This storage of fat can preserve them for over a month, such as in desert areas and when water is scarce.

It is not unusual to see a camel with a deflated hump, which is an indication that the camel needs to take in nourishment to replenish the hump. Naturally, the camels' ability to live extended periods - sometimes months- without a drink of water is its most fascinating adaptation. The life span of a camel is between 40 to 50 years.

Most camels are over 6 feet tall and weigh over 1000 pounds, that is a large species of a hoofed mammal! Camels are known to be gentle, soft, and noble animals who are sacred to those who own them. The camel is a highly intelligent and emotional animal. They form close bonds with their human counterparts and work with a gallant dignity when they are treated with respect.

An interesting fact about camels: since horses are fearful of camels, in ancient times, herds would be used in battle to scare off the enemy's horses and provide victory against armies mounted on horseback. One could say they were a weapon of mass destruction.

These wonderful working animals are suited for their dessert habitat and are a vital means of transportation for both humans and cargos. Camels were created for such weather conditions that most other breeds would not survive. Of particular importance are their feet, which enable them to walk in extremely dry and sandy pathways, the built of their feet keeps them from sinking into the sand. Their genetic breakdown shows the camel has a different shape of red blood cells, unlike other mammals. They have oval-shaped red blood cells (not round) which allows their blood to circulate even in times where dehydration sets in.

The camel is mentioned several times in the Bible, representing many dimensions of the animal and signage, such as wealth, power, and status. For our exploration, we will focus on two incidents. In Genesis 24 we read the instructions from Abraham to his senior servant in his household, the one assigned to everything Abraham had, Abraham told him to go and get a wife for his son, Isaac and to make sure she did not come from the daughters of the

Canaanites, but from Abraham's own country and people; specifically his relatives.

Yes, God uses people and even animals to do his will. Later we read he used a donkey as well. What a mighty God we serve, he is not inconvenienced by any situation to assign his will to any chosen and willing vessel. Thus, the cigarette in my initial introduction could have easily hamper the mission of talking about these heroic creatures.

The story picks up in verses 10-25 (*Genesis 24, NIV*):

> *"Then the servant left, taking with him ten of his master's camels loaded with all kinds of good things from his master. He set out for Aram Naharaim and made his way to the town of Nahor. He had the camels kneel down near the well outside the town; it was toward evening, the time the women go out to draw water.*
>
> *Then he prayed, "LORD, God of my master Abraham, make me successful today, and show kindness to my master Abraham.*
>
> *See, I am standing beside this spring, and the daughters of the townspeople are coming out to draw water. May it be that when I say to a young woman, 'Please let down your jar that I may have a drink,' and she says,*

'Drink, and I'll water your camels too'—let her be the one you have chosen for your servant Isaac. By this I will know that you have shown kindness.

Before he had finished praying, Rebekah came out with her jar on her shoulder. She was the daughter of Bethuel son of Milkah, who was the wife of Abraham's brother Nahor. The woman was very beautiful, a virgin; no man had ever slept with her. She went down to the spring, filled her jar, and came up again.

The servant hurried to meet her and said, "Please give me a little water from your jar."

"Drink, my lord," she said, and quickly lowered the jar to her hands and gave him a drink.

After she had given him a drink, she said, "I'll draw water for your camels too, until they have had enough to drink." So she quickly emptied her jar into the trough, ran back to the well to draw more water, and drew enough for all his camels.

Without saying a word, the man watched her closely to learn whether or not the LORD had made his journey successful.

When the camels had finished drinking, the man took out a gold nose ring weighing a beka and two gold bracelets weighing ten shekels. Then he asked, "Whose daughter are you? Please tell me, is there room in your father's house for us to spend the night?"

She answered him, "I am the daughter of Bethuel, the son that Milkah bore to Nahor." And she added, "We have plenty of straw and fodder, as well as room for you to spend the night."

Detailing the situation, we see a master, a son, a servant, a camel, a wife, and an impending future, all resulting in the legacy of the promise. The servant played a key role in the promise. The son and master did not go out to find the wife, but relied on the servant to produce a 'God-called" outcome.

What is the significance of this servant in this story? Why didn't God cause a great storm to happen, and the outcome was different? Because sometimes 'the thing is not the thing' at all. Sometimes, God will use the circumstances of our situation to bring his plans to pass. At times we will need to see our situation through the eyes of another person. In this case, the master and son had to depend on the third party to complete the cycle. I believe the role of this servant was to activate the next level of the journey. Call upon the helper, in this case, the servant.

A servant is defined as a person who performs duties for others, especially a person employed in a house on domestic duties or as a personal attendant. How critical is that? We see that Jesus came not to be served but to serve (*Matthew 20:28*). He took his assignment in order and judiciously, rebuking those who did not align to God's timing and purpose. After Jesus completed his assignment as the son, he released the 'helper' the Holy Spirit, who would come to serve and perform his duties of being our advocate, our comforter, our guide back to the Son and Master.

Servitude is important to get the will of God accomplished through men. This servant took his duties seriously and attended to his assignment, in agreement with Abraham about the success of the assignment, or what would be considered a success. We see a contrast with Jesus here as we learned that the bible tells us (*1 Peter 1:20*), before the foundation of the world was set, God chose Jesus as our ransom. Jesus knew the terms of the agreement and the impending victory. Jesus asked about the terms of the agreement, down to the release from the oath of the terms of the agreement in his agonizing moments before the physicality of the cross assignment.

The role of the servant in Abraham's household was the link to establishing the fulfillment of God's plan. This was a critical assignment requiring trust and faith in securing the lineage of Abrahams's promise.

141

Remember, the promise was to be accomplished with Isaac in fulfilling the covenant that God made with Abraham, that he would make him the father of many nations, through his son Isaac. The servant (in Abraham's story) likewise negotiated with God on granting his success in his master's instructions. This is how the Holy Spirit operates with us, he negotiates on our behalf and finds us favor with God, the Father. The Holy Spirit is our advocate, our helper, our wisdom applicator in understanding the will of God and the purpose of our being.

The story begins with Abraham and his belief in God, Abraham was granted success in securing a wife for his son Isaac. This required man's obedience; God still waits on man to activate his promise to us. Even with a known outcome, action is still required. The servant must go in pursuit of the assignment to find a bride for Isaac and Jesus still had to physically die on the cross to secure a bride for himself.

God does not take the easy way out (many times, we wish he would), he grows us through the struggles and challenges of daily living. God promised to never leave us nor forsake us, he did not say we would not encounter difficulties. We all must go through our "nevertheless" trials and tests to sometimes win the victory. We must be willing to trust and obey, both believing and knowing that God truly is in control, and nothing escapes his understanding. We must be brave enough to defy our limitations and confront our fears, knowing that God is the master of our destiny and giving him full control to lead and guide us.

This is not always easy, as we have the great adversary (Satan) who is waiting to remind us of our experience or lack thereof, Satan tempts us to rely on those experiences and not trust God. He often makes a great case, because he uses our individual knowledge and experience to show us what our minds often refuse to forget. We must remember that Satan is an excellent worker in his assignment, he comes to steal, kill, and destroy.

In the story, the servant did something so remarkable that we can easily overlook it. He went out of 'self-reliance' and relied on the God of his master, Abraham. He appealed to God to remember his master Abraham and grant him a favor. WOW! The servant knew that he could not do the task set before him but knew "Who" could get it done. I would venture to say that the servant was familiar with the covenant God made with Abraham. The covenant stated that Isaac was to be the lineage to the people God called and will be established to carry out his will. Think about it, Jesus came out of that lineage to seal our victory.

The servant's role was to represent his master and go under the name of his master. He was to represent his master by retelling the exact instructions given to him by his master and the role he was to play. He did not deviate from the plan. Likewise, God has a plan, and his plan will come to pass, it will not tarry or be shortened from the exact time and purpose for which it was created. Jesus has provided us access to the Holy Spirit as a continuation of that plan, who will lead us back to the Master. Part of the assignment of the Holy Spirit is to lead us back to Christ, to see Jesus in the great plan of reconciliation.

Now back to the camel. Remember when we read that the camel can drink up to 40 gallons of water in a matter of minutes? Remember the prayer of the servant in Genesis 24:14 (NIV) *"May it be that when I say to a young woman, 'Please let down your jar that I may have a drink,' and she says, 'Drink, and I'll water your camels too'—let her be the one you have chosen for your servant Isaac. By this I will know that you have shown kindness to my master."* The servant was not only asking for favor for his assignment but also for his camels. What a powerful prayer of confirmation... *Lord if it be you showing me this answered prayer, may my camels also receive favor from this woman.*

Imagine how strong, brave, kindhearted, and trusting Rebekah had to be to fulfill this assignment. This was not an easy job it demanded both a mental shift and physical strength. But we do not see Rebekah complaining how tired she was and why did this stranger come to her path and now wants a drink, not only for himself but for his camels, who can drink 40 gallons of water in a matter of minutes. Can you see this young lady, retrieving water from the brook or well, enough to provide for more than one camel? Even fetching water back/forth for one camel was a back-breaking task. But she did for ten camels! I am in awe of the servant's prayer on what his clue would be that God was with him and he would find favor. This was an impossible task by man's standards, so it had to be God to provide this favor. God still operates in this manner today, he wants to make our impossible prayers, possible through him.

Another fascinating story using the camel as an analogy from the story Jesus told in *Matthew 19:24 (NIV): "Again I say to you, it is easier for a camel to go through the eye of a needle, than for a rich man to enter the kingdom of God."*

Is Jesus saying that it is impossible for rich people to make it to heaven? Absolutely not! This was in reference to a young man who came to Jesus and asked him what must he do to get eternal life? Jesus recited all the commandments and the young man stated that he had kept them, and what does he still lack? Jesus replied, "Go sell all your possessions, give it to the poor and you will have treasures in heaven. Then come and follow me." The Bible says, this young rich man "went away sad because he had great wealth." Upon seeing his reaction and knowing his heart, Jesus made the above statement to his disciples.

We must be careful to not take verses out of context to satisfy our own story or thinking. Having earthly wealth does not prevent a person from getting eternal life. But how wealth is produced, maintained, honored, and idolized can affect our relationship with God. We often hear the quote that money is the root of all evil, when, the actual statement includes *'love of'* money is the root of all evil (*1 Timothy 6:10 NIV*). Some people covet (money) in seeking the satisfaction of this world. Money is just one such evil in covetousness. We can covet in many other ways outside of money, with jobs, hobbies, projects, status, labels, investments, and each other (family/friends/name worshippers).

Here is a version of the story, that Jesus used the camel in this situation due to the audience he was addressing. He was reflecting on a certain gate built on the wall of ancient Jerusalem that was suitable for only pedestrians. It was so small in comparison to the wall that it was called, the 'Needle's eye". A camel could only go through it after it got rid of the items it was carrying and crawled through the passageway. In this case, the camel must have its load (wealth) unloaded to be granted access to the other side. In like manner, if we put other priorities before God, we would have a difficult time in having our undivided attention focused on God. That is the importance of *Matthew 6:33 (KJV)*: *"But seek ye first the kingdom of God, and his righteousness; and all these things shall be added onto you".* Gods' desire for us is all the good things the earth has to offer, but he must be the center of our hearts. He repeatedly told the Israelite children; thou shall have no other gods before me. He insisted on being first in their life. He is the same God yesterday, today, and forever and as a result demands the same of us, his children.

Jesus was reminding this young man to put God first above all his possession and he will be increased ever the more. Jesus told him to, "come and follow me." He did not tell him that having earthly possessions was not necessary, but he wanted to see where his heart was. Money (or wealth) is not the issue but our attachment to it is. It can cause our inconsistency in following God. We can be blinded to think God is placing a demand on the things we have and the expectation from God regarding those things. Where is truly our heart, who or what owns our focus?

Just like in the case of the camel, it was not that the camel was being denied access to the other side of the gate. But to access that provision, he was to unload his treasures (his test) and once he passes through (his victory), he could be rewarded and continue with his journey. The camel had to trust by unloading, it could then get on its knees to the other side, then reload to continue with its assignment. We need to unload our burdens (often our tests), the things that keep us up all night, robbing us of precious energy and sapping our strength, to carry on with the days' assignment. Because we are too scared to unload, we walk away sad, thinking that God is demanding too much of us.

Whether the story reflects an actual wall built in Jerusalem and what the camel needed to do to be granted access or not, wealth itself was not the problem but our attachment to it. Some have taken the opposite view considering this scripture to mean that God wants his people to be poor and have no appearance of earthly wealth attached to their names for the exterior manifestation of godliness. If we are to be poor in this world, we will appear better than those with physical goods and somehow make it to heaven by this avenue. That poverty gives him some sort of piety. Again, we can use scripture to support our views but we need to be mindful and seek the Spirit's guidance.

The Bible tells us, *"Be not deceived; God is not mocked: for whatsoever a man soweth, that shall he also reap."* *Galatians 6:7 (KJV).* We do not achieve salvation through our own means, rather it is a gift from God. Someone who loves the world whether rich or poor will not be in Gods' kingdom.

Observation Point: Every detail God has imparted to us is of importance. God is in the details of his plan for our life. He did not leave anything to chance. He has and continues to use any vessel of choice to accomplish his plan. God has provided us some of the secrets of His plan, when we can be fully trusted with the source, his grace is provided in the revelations provided to man. When reflecting on the many examples that our great and powerful Father has used to open our eyes and ears, I am amazed at the many blessings He has bestowed upon His people. We get to examine and learn from the plethora of nuggets left for us in His goodness. We get to learn and glean not from our own understanding but to rely on the unlimited wisdom of God. He has not left us powerless but with the guidance of the Holy Spirit, we can understand more of the gracious demonstrations of God.

The work of the camel is significant. We saw that God can use any instrument to carry out His plan. This gives me such comfort knowing that God's plan will come to fruition, we can trust the process to completion. How about you, can you take God at His word and continue to push through no matter what it looks like in the natural?

<u>Reader's Notes</u>: *Embrace the Message Within*

_____

_____

_____

_____

_____

_____

_____

_____

_____

_____

_____

_____

_____

Chapter 9
BUTTERFLY

L et me tell you a quick story. When I was a child, I loved trying to catch butterflies. I would gather all the mason and empty jelly jars that I could find and then would add a handful of grass to make their new home as comfortable as possible. I would poke tiny holes in the lid with a fork or knife so that they could breathe when I captured them. Then I would patiently wait until they would land on the ground, on leaves, or on a flower before attempting to grab it. If I couldn't catch them with my fingers as they lay on the ground, then I would get creative and other measures were taken. It was always challenging running through the wide vacant lots or fields with some long tree branches to swap them to the ground. I can still see the colorful powder/dust from their wings that would get on my fingers as I captured them.

I found it fascinating watching the butterflies flap their wings against the glass jar. Eventually, they would give up and rest on the grass inside of it. Then I would unscrew the lid to set them free. There were many times they wouldn't fly out. It looked as though they were used to being captured, surrendered, and then accepted their fate. I recall flicking the jar to motivate them, wake them up, as I anticipated their flight. If there wasn't any movement or any effort on their part, I would turn the jar upside down to force them to fly free.

There were numerous times the butterfly flew out of the jar just to lay lifeless on the grass. I would gently touch or poke their wings to encourage them to fly away. Some butterflies would realize they were no longer in the jar and free to fly away. And sadly, there were other times the butterflies would die from being captured in the jar. I honestly thought I provided them with what they needed. I never could figure out why some lived, and others died. I never wanted to harm any butterflies that would fly so freely in the air, or land on flowers. My intention, focus, and challenge were only to capture them, watch them, and let them go.

A few months ago, when I was taking a walk on my thinking path, I found a rock painting of a butterfly. I was surprised by the different emotions that stirred up inside of me. These same emotions brought me back to when I was a child and would see those beautiful and unique butterflies flying around or landing gracefully on a plant. Stay with me, as we take flight into my childhood. Any sight of a butterfly causes me to reminisce of that carefree child in me. That child who loved running through vacant fields with long broken tree branches, uncontrollable, and determined to capture these fluttering creations. That innocent fearless child without any care or concerns except to catch butterflies.

As I grow older, I now see butterflies as insightful examples of life experiences. The transformation and process from a caterpillar that becomes a beautiful butterfly. A cocoon-like a mother's womb shielding her unborn baby as it goes through the process of development until it's time to be welcomed into this world; or the childhood stages, like a caterpillar growing into its life's purpose and reaches its final transformation as a butterfly.

We are not created to remain a caterpillar that crawls on the ground for others to squash us. We are destined to fly! Yes, my friend, the free will to just fly freely and land on things that nurture us as we grow in life to nurture others. If we are not careful, bad decisions in life can make us captive and kill our dreams.

Who would have known that the butterfly would impact my life so much as a child that its effects and very nature transformed the way I witnessed my late mother and sister's life? The most important women in my life, both exhibited beautiful transformations in each season of their lives. They are my human butterflies. Every time I see a butterfly, it's my sign, my God wink. Crazy as it may sound, it brings me comfort and a smile.

As a young adult, I watched my mother, Marion, live a life of fear and insecurity. It could have been the era she grew up in and lived, but she underestimated herself in many things, yet she was strong, bold, and encouraged others. A stay-at-home mother during that period, in the 1950's, felt her purpose or contribution in life wasn't as exciting nor grand as the other women that worked outside of the home. Back then, being a stay-at-home mother was the norm, but without much recognition. My mother's positive attitude impacted many lives throughout her lifetime. Even though she may not have fully grasped the effect she had on others, I have known and heard so many people share how she made a difference that impacted their life so much that their lives were altered and were never the same.

A few weeks before her death, her ultimate transition, I witnessed a total transformation in my mothers' mind and body. Have you ever witnessed someone do a full 180 degree turn right before your own eyes? It was mind-blowing and powerful! In this case, her 180 enhanced the beauty that I already knew and took it to another level. It was like she came into herself with confidence and peace, and it filled the atmosphere. I witness a caterpillar go into a cocoon and transformed into a fearless, determined, pain-free, and focused butterfly of a mom. I learned so much about my mother upon her transition from Earth to Heaven. When she was ready to go to her heavenly home, my butterfly of a mother, was vibrant. She was fearless and excited with anticipation of leaving this earth to be with God. Her love for God was evident and unwavering. I saw the full and real her; the evolution from cocoon to a butterfly that finally realized she could fly.

These scriptures along with her prayers truly came alive in her life. Her favorite scripture,

Psalm 27: 1(KJV): "The LORD is my light and salvation; whom shall, I fear? The LORD is the strength of my life; of whom shall I be afraid?" and *Psalm 27:14 (KJV): "Wait on the LORD: be of good courage, and he shall strengthen thine heart: wait, I say on the LORD."*

I would hear my mother recite these scriptures over-and-over again. These scriptures brought peace, heart transformation, courage, and anticipation with knowing her eternal life was drawing near. My butterfly of a mother's love for God, family, and friends was immeasurable. Her presence will forever be embedded in my heart and all the lives she touched with her integrity and love which will forever leave a powerful and impactful legacy for her family and others.

My butterfly sister, Clarita always had a free spirit. To me, she was always so strong, independent, and easy to confide in. She was always dedicated and practiced personal self-awareness. As a child, she traveled with her mind to places by reading numerous books. And when she got older, she took her body to those places and experienced them firsthand. Clarita used her words wisely, always supported and encouraged herself as well as others. She lived life full and died empty. My butterfly sister kept moving forward to avoid being captured by the lies that life tried to clip her wings. Clarita is one of those butterflies in my life that represents freedom.

I believe many people at one point in their life experienced a season that felt wrapped, trapped, or covered up like being inside of a cocoon. They may not have realized the lid was removed. All they had to do is fly. Everyone has a choice to surrender and believe the limitations of their environment. But we can simply adjust, reassess, and never surrender to what it may look like. We can fight for a new outcome and rise above any present circumstances that will not hold us captive.

Always be aware of a little girl with a glass jar! Someone is always watching. Like the caterpillar going into the cocoon to transform into a butterfly. My hope is that everyone could look back on their lives to see some form of change even though we do not develop and mature at the same pace.

Transformation starts within the mind. We read in *Romans 12:2 (NIV): "Do not conform to the pattern of this*

*world, but be transformed by the renewing of your mind.
Then you will be able to test and approve what God's will is-
his good, pleasing and perfect will."*

The Bible tells us about being influenced by differences of opinions and advice. I believe there have been incidents in your life, like mine, where someone has given good advice, but at times we are not ready to receive it. That advice was probably heard, but not fully understood. Some people's motives may be honorable, but without understanding and being ready to receive it, means nothing. If my mind isn't changed then there isn't transformation.

Observation Point: The word of God is alive. With God, you are always more than enough. Let me tell you that again, YOU are enough. He knows and sees you as He created you to be. Unfortunately, because we do not see it, we don't believe it. We like to believe we know more than we do. We believe we are in control, but it is not so. Let's look at this from a spiritual perspective.

I always knew that God was there. My relationship with Him was important. I don't know a life without Him. So, for me, reading the bible and surrendering my ways of thinking, doing things, responding to His guidance should bring an unmeasurable outcome. I can see how the rest of the scripture states to test and approve your change. God is unchanging but we are. God is consistent but we change and go with the tides and times. However, we are created in His image, and we should be able to reflect His unchanging image. And that starts with a transformation of our mindset.

Reader's Notes: *Embrace the Message Within*

Chapter 10
HOPE

Hope on a rock. How reflective and telling is that? Hope is often viewed as softer, pliable, bendable, flexible, after all it is descriptive of something to come, not here yet the beginning of something in the present. Although not touchable, it expresses a knowing of our possibilities. So even seeing the word, 'hope' captured on a rock produced a positive reaction. A reminder, so to speak, of light to come. Seeing 'hope' speaking back to me on that rock, formed my view of the day ahead, it was a hope-filled day.

The Bible invites us to reflect on hope as the confidence of an expectation being fulfilled, through our Lord Christ Jesus. Hope is the expected outcome of the Lord's promise. Therefore, we place our hope in Christ Jesus, the one who anchors the fulfillment of the expected outcome.

According to Merriam-Webster dictionary:

"Hope" is to cherish a desire with anticipation: to want something to happen to be true: to desire with expectation of obtainment or fulfillment: and to expect with confidence: to trust.

Both naturally and spiritually speaking, hope is positive and has the potential to pull us through difficult times. As believers in Christ, our hope is founded on Him who never changes and this knowledge is lifechanging. We are anchored on the hope of Jesus Christ who is steadfast, complete, redemptive, eternal; the same yesterday, today, and forevermore. We often hear this referred to as having our 'blessed hope in Christ.'

What is the hope Jesus referred us to radiate? God wants us, as his children, to have our hope in him. *Deuteronomy 31:6 (ESV)*, instructs us to *"Be strong and courageous. Do not fear or be in dread of them, for it is the LORD your God who goes with you. He will not leave you or forsake you."*

In his transition of leadership of the children of Israel to Joshua, Moses was encouraging the Israelites to have their hope in God. While Moses would not be leading them into the promised land, God was the one who all along was their provider and had already fought and prepared their destiny ahead. They were to remain strong and courageous. Remain hopeful.

Likewise, the Lord will go with us and has promised to never leave or forsake us. No matter how the situation screams at us that we are alone, we can take the promise of God as truth. God does not make empty promises. God says to walk boldly *'do not fear or be in dread'* into our destiny which has been prepared for us. Fear is False Evidence Appearing Real. God urges us to walk through it, He will be with us. Do you know that fear is the devil's spirit, our enemy?

The enemy would have us believe the limited view of fear. Fear has no future unless we give it one by taking it with us. That does not mean fear does not exist, because it does, but it is saying do not allow fear to take residency in our situation. Fear only lasts when we allow it to, fear will not move out if we keep nurturing and providing comfort to the atmosphere for it to breed.

Fear gets comfortable when we create the perfect environment for it to flourish. Do not be ruled by fear but look to the One who has planned our success. Once we look fear in the eye and firmly proclaim we are the righteousness of God in Christ Jesus, then fear must go. Now fear is like its image bearer, the devil, it will move on but that does not mean it will not wait for another opportune moment to try again. We must keep rebuking fear and trusting God. One way to do this is to believe that the Lord our God goes with us.

God never expects us to embark on the journey by ourselves. He promises if we do our part, He will do his part. Our part is to be strong and courageous, do not fear, believe that God has a plan for each of us and that He will not leave us to accomplish it by ourselves. If we align to God's plan for our life, it will always lead to our success. God knows the plans He has for us (Jeremiah 29:11). He asks us to walk in that knowledge with Him.

Does the manufacturer of a finished product intentionally create a defect in its product? No, the manufacturer knows intimately the products' potential and the best way to make it work. God is our creator (our manufacturer), who knows exactly what outcome he included in the operation of his product (his children). The way we work God's plan is to operate in the intent of His plan, his expected results. As we align to His will, we see the expected outcome for that prosperous future He promised us.

When we walk in fellowship with God, we wait to hear His instructions on our next move. *Psalm 39:7 (ESV)* says, *"And now, O Lord, for what do I wait? My hope is in you."'* Here is where the children of Israel and most of us often miss it, the waiting process. We are so anxious for God to hurry up and fulfill our wishes and desires, that we do not process the waiting period as just that...wait. We want to assist God by providing him a solution that we think will fix our situation, then when that goes wrong, we end up with our own solution and blame God.

Out of our mouths can come comments like; God is not for me; God no longer listens to my needs; perhaps that was not what God told me to begin with; I wonder if God hears and even sees me. With such thoughts our confidence in God starts to diminish and we question his goodness towards us. When our confidence diminishes in the source of our hope, we start to doubt. Therefore, a huge part of hope is waiting. Hope can only be hope if it is an expectation to come, an outlook that gives us encouragement in the now.

God reminds us that those that wait upon Him will renew their strength. How do we renew our strength? By the hope that is in us when we anchor our expectation in the consistency of God's promise. That promise comes with the conditions of God's plans. While we do not have to perform to receive the conditions of Gods' love, goodness, grace, and mercy, we are subject to the conditions of His promise. We absolutely must do our part to receive the promises of God, according to his will. We know that God is not a man that He should lie and that His promises reflect His justice. For us to employ the promises of God we need to fulfill the conditions of that promise. There are many promises in the word of God and each has conditions for its fulfillment.

We are quick to quote scriptures that lay hold of the promise of God without the context and content of the promise. There is a cause and effect of the promise of God. One common scripture I hear overused is in reference to being the head and not the tail, "I am the head and not the tail". If we look at that scripture in an expanded view it reads as such, *"The LORD will make you the head, not the tail. If you pay attention to the commands of the LORD your God that I give you this day and carefully follow them, you will always be at the top, never at the bottom."* Deuteronomy 28:13 (NIV).

There is an "if" clause to that transitional expression. If we obey and follow Gods' commands, then he is establishing a covenant with us to the promise of the outcome. Let us be careful in our acknowledging view of our Heavenly Father. If not, we can easily subject our view of God to being a genie from a bottle, which may result in an attitude of blaming God for not giving us what we desire when the truth is that we have not done our part of the agreement.

When we wait on God, our hope is indeed secured in Him, else our hope can be cut off from its source. From *Proverbs 24:14 (ESV),* we learn to *"Know that wisdom is such to your soul; if you find it, there will be a future, and your hope will not be cut off".*

To neglect the wisdom of hope is to be removed from the potential of our purpose. The only way to truly find our purpose is to incorporate the spiritual wisdom of God and to know the mind of God. The book of Proverbs is known as one of the great books of wisdom in the Bible. Others in which is demonstrated the practicality of hope is the books of Ecclesiastes and Job. While we will not explore these books here, there is no way to know the hope of God without some exploration of the wisdom of God as defined in the book of Job (*which the reader is encouraged to read*).

As we build an intimate relationship with God, we learn to find the wisdom in God. Throughout scripture, wisdom serves as an application in modeling hope. Without an understanding of the source and implications of the scriptures, our hope would be reduced to mere human understanding. The first chapter of Proverbs talks about the fear (reverence) of the Lord as the beginning of knowledge, but "fools despise wisdom and instructions."

In my own personal walk with God, I did not begin to understand the wisdom of God without first acknowledging the hope contained within my expectations concerning His wisdom. The word of God contains his wisdom and instructions for an expected outcome. There is much hope within the promises of God, without which I would be defeated. For example, whenever my body starts to ache, I remember the promise of healing and that I am covered by the healing blood of Jesus. This gives me hope of my expected healing. Even if I do not immediately feel any different, I am confident of His words. That is my hope, the anchor to my expectation.

On my own, I am limited by my thoughts, my ever-changing emotions, my experiences, my mind, my heart, my humanness. As such, I call upon the wisdom revealed and modeled by those who, likewise, had a similar hope. The scriptures contain documented hope expressed by those saints before us. The wisdom of God as shared by them creates in me a new perspective as I too build my hope on God and surrender my heart and life to Him.

There is that hope of glory, to reflect God's goodness and encourage others to place their hope in Him, especially when we see the opposite of goodness, mercy, and grace in our world. While we are living in the world, let us be consistent in the hope of God and not be cut off from the wisdom of that hope.

As we are reminded in the book of *Isaiah 40:31 (ESV),* *"But they who wait for the Lord shall renew their strength; they shall mount up with wings like eagles; they shall run and not be weary; they shall walk and not faint."* I remember as a child hearing that scripture verse as a song and always loving the picture it created in my mind. Flying is one of those 'superpowers' I always wanted to be gifted with if I had such a wish. I suppose it is more due to my impatience and wanting something quickly. I must admit, I am still a work in progress on that one. Thank God for grace!

I recalled thinking, if only I could fly like a bird, what would it feel like to be so free, getting from one area to another quickly. My favorite dreams were those that involved me flying and doing summersaults through the clouds. They were fantastic and I would always be disappointed when I woke up. That's possibly why I wanted to be a flight attendant in my younger years as well.

If you study the eagle, it is admired for its endurance and ability to rise above new heights to safety. The eagle has the innate ability to keep moving against the storm to carry its eaglets to a sanctuary away from predators. God often described his intent towards Israel as their protector, beginning with their deliverance from Egyptian slavery. God carried them through the wilderness to the safety of the promised land.

God even provided them with the hope of being his treasured possession if they obeyed and kept his covenant. God had the perfect plan and had already provided for their success. It did come with an 'if...then' condition because He is a just God. God wants us to be like eagles, flying against the storms of life, soaring to new heights because we too have a protector.

In the above passage, the prophet Isaiah is communicating the promise that God will provide renewed strength and courage (hope) to overcome obstacles if Israel would only have patience and trust in the Lord's sovereign timing. Likewise, we can have the same hope in God by obeying and accepting the covenant fulfilled by Jesus Christ on our behalf. We serve the same unchanging God. We too are to wait faithfully on God.

In having the hope and waiting on Him, we find that we too will mount up with wings like an eagle, as our strength, power, courage, and patience increases. The verse concludes by reminding us of actions necessary to the fulfillment of that promise; we are to run and walk and not give up, never to faint even when we get weary. Our hope and anchor remain in God, He will do the lifting, but we also have a part in the partnership; building of our relationship with Him.

When done according to Gods' pattern, we learn in *Romans 5:5 (ESV), "And hope does not put us to shame, because God's love has been poured into our hearts through the Holy Spirit who has been given us.'"* The Bible tells us that the hope we have in God will not disappoint us, we will not be put to shame, because of God's ability, integrity, and power to love us beyond measure. Our ability to love, honor, and trust God, stems from His love being poured into our hearts by His Holy Spirit who enables us to respond. We cannot have hope in someone that does not mean anything to us. That would be a futile exercise of disappointment.

Romans 8:24-25 (ESV) reminds us of the love that leads us to a blessed hope. *"For in this hope we are saved. Now hope that is seen is not hope. For who hopes for what he sees? But if we hope for what we do not see, we wait for it with patience."* Hope is an unseen. We hope in what is unseen as soon as it is seen it is no longer hope. I find that fascinating because hope teaches us to wait, then that manifests in increased patience.

As a practical means, we are always to be with hope, our expectation anchored in God. Hope fulfilled is no longer hope but a triumphant reward. The development of hope yields Gods' provisions. As a result, we are to *'rejoice in hope, be patient in tribulation, and constant in prayer,' Romans 12:12 (ESV)*.

The Bible states that hope brings us to a position of rejoicing. Think of it this way, we cannot experience two separate emotions at the same time, if we are in a position of expectancy (hope) and thereby rejoicing, then we are no longer focused on the position of lack (the absence of hope).

The instruction of obedience produces hope, *"For whatever was written in former days was written for our instruction, that through endurance and through the encouragement of the scriptures we might have hope." Romans 15:4 (ESV).* We have evidence of those individuals who have captured their hope documented in scriptures, to encourage our hearts to hope. So that we can be filled with all the joy and peace in believing God and our hope may be increased by the power of the Holy Spirit who brings about the fulfillment of our hope.

There are so many points of reference in scripture on the importance of hope because God knows the human spirit can easily be distracted and give up hope of better things to come. *2 Corinthians 4:16-18 (ESV)* puts it this way, *"So we do not lose heart. Though our outer self is wasting away, our inner self is being renewed day by day. For this light momentary affliction is preparing for us an eternal weight of glory beyond all comparison, as we look not to the things that are seen but to the things that are unseen. For the things that are seen are transient, but the things that are unseen are eternal."*

Our hope is not in this world's offerings, but in the promises of God that secures our eternal life. The world offers many mirages in the hope of enticing our hearts, but only God can comfort and provide the hope of a better tomorrow.

We have this promise in *Colossians 1:27 (ESV), "To them God chose to make known how great among the Gentiles are the riches of the glory of this mystery, which is Christ in you, the hope of glory."'*

We can easily become discouraged with the hope of this world because it is temporary. Here today and gone tomorrow, thereby the level of stress this creates is constant and detrimental to both our physical and emotional health.

Hope placed in the wrong source has disastrous results, creating an unhealthy image of self. With our hope anchored in Christ, we have the hope of his glory, the riches of the mystery that can only be satisfied in the knowledge of who Christ is, in the mystery of his revelations.

We are reminded in *1 Timothy 6:17 (ESV)*, *"As for the rich in this present age, charge them not to be haughty, nor to set their hopes on the uncertainty of riches, but on God, who richly provides us with everything to enjoy."* Did you catch that? This is a phenomenal promise. Let us not be enticed with the riches of the world and as a result get arrogant, proud, superior, stuck-up, puffed up, self-important, conceited, snooty, self-aggrandizing, overconfident, condescending, high and mighty, supposing something we are not. Rather, let us set our hope on God, who has true riches and provides us with everything needed to enjoy his endless riches.

It can be tempting to feel secure with the promises of this world, when seeking the comfort and pleasures the world tells us will provide happiness. The truth is that this is temporary and as soon as that 'it' is satisfied, we want something else to take 'its' place. The world's offerings can never be enjoyable, it is short-term and short-lived. On the other hand, *"We have this as a sure and steadfast anchor of the soul, a hope that enters into the inner place behind the curtain,"* *Hebrews 6:19 (ESV)*. To be steadfast is to be unwavering, committed, firm, dedicated, and resolute.

Our hope in God promises all these attributes as an affirmation of this hope. It is an anchor of the soul. The soul is where we have our will, our emotions, our intellect. Our souls can be anchored in that inner place with God seeing we are no longer separated by the ancient curtain that separated the Most-High Priest and granted access to the Holy of Holies only once a year. We have been emancipated and granted access directly to our God. Our hope is in Him and not someone else taking our pleas, petitions, prayers of praise beyond the curtain for us. Our hope in God is sure, secure, fixed, and safe; we are well-founded in Him.

There is no shame in our confession of our hope in Christ. *"Let us hold fast the confession of our hope without wavering, for he who promised is faithful." Hebrews 10:23 (ESV).* In the area of hope, there are two specific things we can depend on God for: 1. the *integrity* of His word, and 2. the *power* to carry it out. *Isaiah 55:11 (NIV)* says, *"So is my word that goes out from my mouth: It will not return to me empty, but will accomplish what I desire and achieve the purpose for which I sent it."* As God says it, so He will establish it.

To hold fast to a promise of God means we can cling, stick, and hang on to it. God is not a man that He should lie. God owes man nothing, yet has provided for us our every need even prior to our creation. When we read the first chapter of the book of Genesis, we understand the measurement of God's perfect plan for our life. God is faithful to His promises. We have a hope that is foundational to our very existence, there are no desires of man that God has not provided for.

Therefore, we can rest assured of placing our hope in an Almighty God that left nothing to chance and created order for our benefit. We are reminded in In *Hebrews 11:1 (ESV)*, *"Now faith is the assurance of things hoped for, the conviction of things not seen."* Looks like we cannot have faith unless we have hope. The evidence of faith is the hope we have of its truth. Hope produces faith, hope is the other side of faith, they are mirrored images of each other. They exist side by side, one supporting the other. The same way we cannot count to five unless we get to four then five, we cannot get to faith, unless we have hope. Faith is the assurance of our hope. But we need to have hope first and then faith comes to support our position of hope.

I was pondering on this verse and realized the intentionality of God and how orderly he truly is. It took me to the stories of the last born given more authority over the firstborn. The examples of Esau selling his birthright to Jacob, Joseph receiving the double portion blessings of the firstborn (which should have gone to Reuben), Seth mentioned as Adam's lineage and not Cain, Rebecca being the favorite wife of Jacob (as opposed to Leah, the older daughter), and even David as the chosen king over Israel, as opposed to his older brothers. All these remind me that God has the purpose to his plans. We may not understand but He knows best and never needs to answer to us.

There are no errors in the provision of God, only willing vessels as he has so ordained. With freewill we are allowed to choose. Hope does not have to supersede faith, but is it God's order? The Bible tells us faith is the assurance of things hoped for, God is not a man that he should lie. We take God at his word, that is the basis of our hope. Again, faith is the assurance of our hope. And as each has been provided a measure of faith, we do have the ability to exercise hope.

Hope was activated by the revelatory grace of our Lord and Savior Jesus Christ. We have not experienced the balance of our future provisions, but we accept it as truth because of the hope we have in Jesus. Hope in Christ does not happen on its own, it takes a preparation process that takes us from natural knowing to supernatural knowing. The Bible says, *"Therefore, preparing your minds for action, and being sober-minded, set your hope fully on the grace that will be brought to you at the revelation of Jesus Christ,"'1 Peter 1:13 (ESV).*

What does it mean to be sober-minded? We may falsely believe that we need to be out of our minds to have hope in a promise we have only heard about. We might even justify it by asking the question as the Jews did in the book of Acts, 'are these people drunk so early in the morning to be talking like this?'

But let me assure you that God does not expect us to provide any justification for our hope in Him. He wants us to be prepared in our actions, be sober-minded. We are to be clearheaded, restrained, and temperate in our hope; nothing that demonstrates a chance encounter, but a solid knowing of the revelations on the grace that comes in the hope of Jesus Christ. We do not need to explain our hope, simply we are to remain confident on who anchors our hope.

Confidence in the hope of God takes spending time to get to know him. How can we be expected to have hope in someone we do not know about? Spending time communicating with God through prayer, reading His word, and hearing from Him will build our hope in Him. While we do not need to defend God, we do need to have a relationship with Him to express the hope that we have in Him. *1 Peter 3:15 (ESV)* puts it this way, *"But in your hearts honor Christ the Lord as holy, always being prepared to make a defense to anyone who asks you for a reason for the hope that is in you; yet do it with gentleness and respect."'*

While we do not need to explain our hope, we are to be prepared to defend it. Just like the Apostle Peter was on the day of Pentecost (read Acts 2:14-36), when accused of being drunkards, Apostle Peter was quick to provide a revelation of Jesus to the crowd. Apostle Peter was saying, 'if you do not understand or know who we are acknowledging let me give you some background information and enlighten you on the reason for our actions.' Apostle Peter provided a concrete historical accounting to include what was being witnessed with the crowd.

Apostle Peter was no longer the same disciple who followed Jesus, ready to defend himself, but had now had the hope of Jesus revealed to him and was able to share via that new insight to those who were thirsty for more. Hope brings the fulfillment of the promise of God. Apostle Peter was able to reference both history, recent happenings, and his newfound freedom in Christ. Prior to that, he was hiding and secretly meeting to discuss Jesus. Now, he had boldness in the hope that was now being fulfilled.

Scripture tells us Jesus is the same yesterday, today, and forever. We too can have the same hope in Him, he is no respecter of persons to those truly desiring to know Him. Our hope is in Christ, he is the author and perfecter of our hope and in Him does our hope reside. We do not go about this hope with boasting and disrespect, but we do it with gentleness and respect.

Our actions are to be reflective of Gods' character, with humility, compassion, and extending the mercy and grace of our Lord and Savior, Jesus Christ. Hope is a powerful ingredient in the outspreading of our love towards each other.

Observation Point: Life often hands us choices, one of which is having hope or not having hope. We get to choose as an individual. While we can attempt to hope for another person, it is not the same as that person having hope for themselves. At the end of the day, we each make the decision on who, what, where, how, and why our hope resides on a particular factor. Jesus asks us to have the hope of glory. A hope that is outside our limited thinking and relies on His provision. Tomorrow's outcome is not promised by anything man can provide because man's actions (or lack thereof) are based on emotions, our experience, our knowledge, our intellect, all of which involve human limitations.

Consider those options and make your decision as to whom you would like to have your foundational hope housed. *Proverbs 13:12 (ESV),* it says, *"Hope deferred makes the heart sick, but a desire fulfilled is a tree of life."* Placing our hope in Jesus will indeed yield a longing fulfilled life.

<u>Reader's Notes</u>: *Embrace the Message Within*

_____

_____

_____

_____

_____

_____

_____

_____

_____

_____

_____

_____

_____

Chapter 11

THE HEART OF CHRIST - PAY IT FORWARD

A special piece of our rock discoveries was one that stated, Pay it Forward. The message was so simple yet so powerful. It captures the concept of the Great Commission, to go and make disciples. We see this as the heart of Christ, to leave the 99 and go after the one. Reach back and provide a hope for that one who needs strengthening. Jesus state this to Apostle Peter, to be the hope that strengthens his brothers in the life ahead, feed His sheep.

One of the benefits of achievement is the opportunity to pay it forward by encouraging someone else. The Bible reminds us to remember our small beginnings. *"Do not despise these small beginnings, for the Lord rejoices to see the work begin..." (Zechariah 4:10, NLT).*

Reaching back takes intentionality. To most of us, we are on course with a mindset towards the future, we are looking for the next goal to advance. Imagine getting to a place where you promised yourself you would never look back and then choosing to look back. That is intentionality, which is what paying it forward is all about. You are choosing to remember the journey to your success. In paying it forward we embrace what it took to get to our destination. Without those reminders we often break our character in honoring God.

When men choose to self-direct and not recognize the many individuals on the path of our journey to our destiny, our result can only be external gratification. I remembered asking God one day why I had to suffer and go through so many periods of rejection and dejection. Some of my many insecurities were not feeling loved, I was not good enough to land that job, I was not educated and talented enough for that project, intimidated to speak in public, my words were not good enough to be expressed, not being a marriage material, the list went on and on. Confident? I was not by any means.

I heard God say that I was the opposite of all those things I was saying to myself. He then asked me who was the source of my information about myself. In other words, who was I listening to, because obviously, that was the basis of my belief. More importantly, He asked me what He does say about me.

It was during this uncertainty; I became curious to discover what exactly God did say about me. After all, I was a believer and a follower of Jesus. I began a journey of self-discovery that has not only changed my outlook on myself but also enabled me to help others 'see' who God says they are. I love seeing the look on their faces as I share the love of God and encourage them in their self-discovery on what God says of them as His child.

I have learned that our circumstances assist with our growth, and our assignment is to help the many destined to cross our paths. They too would have some of the same questions and I am now able to exemplify victory while standing in the gap on the way to their victory. I would then have the confidence to provide encouragement because I too, once upon a time, was in the same situation. I did not understand the totality of that assignment at that time, I could only relate to the immediate pain and uncertainty.

God has a perfect plan and definitely continues to use my many uncircumcised situations to mold me towards my 'nevertheless' moments. Every day I continue to be amazed by God and His calling for my life. He shows up in the smallest of assignments because nothing is too small for Him to make my joy unspeakable.

I once was lost but thank God he never lost sight of me. He was there all along my journey, I just could not hear him due to the many distractions in my path. I was longing to belong to this earth, not knowing the earth belongs to me. I had it reversed. God had given me dominion and authority over the earth, and it was already built within my capacity to that ownership.

I came fully loaded for the plans God had designed specifically for me. Everything I will ever need to complete my God-given assignment is already built in me, fully pre-coded, nothing missing, nothing lacking, nothing broken. God does not do anything halfway. It is already completed with God.

Imagine having a property paid for, you have full access to the place, with all the amenities that come with it, utilities paid, well furnished, comfortable rooms, supportive staff, food at your disposal, clothing provided in multiple closets, extra money to spend, and on your dying bed it is then you discovered those benefits belonged to you, all expenses paid. The property was there all along, but you never knew it belonged to you. You saw the property, but never inquired who it belonged to, much less considered it could be yours.

All your life you lived in poverty, not knowing there was a Will out there with your name on it, you were legally entitled to all the provisions of that Will. You heard about a great rich aunt of yours and simply dismissed her existence. Too late, you cannot enjoy any of it now. How sad would that be, you may even wish you could live a little longer, but your body is wracked with pain till death seems as the best and only outcome. At this point, you welcome it quickly. Sadly, many of us are in this exact situation, our Heavenly Father has a plan for our life and has promised us the keys to His kingdom, but we are not sure we can trust the promise. We choose the temporary offerings of this world.

God had already completed the vessel within us, and our assignment was to position ourselves for his purpose so we can discover the plan he had for us before it is too late. God said in *Jeremiah 29:11 (NIV): "For I know the plans I have for you, declares the LORD, plans to prosper you and not to harm you, plans to give you hope and a future."* Can you even begin to imagine the magnitude of that plan? We could not begin to imagine the details of Gods' plan for our life, yet the devil comes to entice us with the worldly materials of this earth. He is the foe, the enemy in disguise of Gods' plan for our life.

Gods' plan will involve the opportunity to grow us, which can come with earthly discomforts, yet He assures us that He will never leave us nor forsake us. Those discomforts are to increase our capacity of endurance, to finish our race by learning to trust and obey. Our pain and sufferings help to build our character, in turn, our character builds our legacy. I want my legacy to define the glory of God in my life. I want my label to reflect God's character, His understanding, His compassion, His kindness, and His endless love.

Let our truths be God's endless truths. His righteousness is our righteousness, not because we can ever be righteous but because we are truly righteous through the blood of Jesus. Let us endure to finish our race that we may hear our Master say, 'well done thou good and faithful servant'. The race involves practice, tests, trials, setbacks, victories, enlightenments, revelations, and the wisdom to keep pressing forward.

The race involves paying it forward as Jesus did with his disciples. He prepared, positioned, and commissioned them to make additional disciples. In other words, be productive and multiply upon the face of the Earth. *Matthew 28:18–20 (NIV)* contains what has come to be called the Great Commission: *"Then Jesus came to them and said, 'All authority in heaven and on earth has been given to me. Therefore, go and make disciples of all nations, baptizing them in the name of the Father and of the Son and of the Holy Spirit, and teaching them to obey everything I have commanded you. And surely, I am with you always, to the very end of the age.'"*

Have you ever asked God what is your purpose, why were you created, what assignment He has for you? This verse in Matthew 28 pretty much sums it up for us all, the how of our individual assignment in getting this command done is our specific deviation based on the diverse talents God has placed in us, but we all have the same assignment, to increase the Kingdom of God. I encouraged you to read the story of the parable of the talents in *Matthew 25:14-30 (ESV)*. Verse 15 states, *"To one he gave five talents. to another two, to another one, to each according to his ability. Then he went away."* God has placed within each of us talents to do His will.

Jesus said all authority in heaven and earth has been given to him, and God has given mankind all authority on earth. We are reminded in the disciples' prayer that we are to pray, "thy kingdom come thy will be done on earth as it is in heaven." Seems like we are being granted authority by Jesus to pray under this covering authority.

Matthew 25:19 states, "therefore, go and make disciples _(pay it forward)_ of all nations." I have often heard when I see the word 'therefore' in scripture to look backward in the text to see what proceeded the word. What is it there for (combined yields 'therefore')? Is there an action or position necessary preceding that word? We have been granted authority to make additional disciples, our response now is to go. Because we have authority, we are to go forth and take the necessary action.

Jesus never wanted the disciples to move until they were equipped to do so. The same is true for us. We are to allow the Holy Spirit to prepare us so we too can go and make disciples in the name of Jesus.

I find it remarkable that most of Jesus' directions were quite simple in understanding, he often said, 'go', 'come', 'follow me', 'out', never the need to complicate his directives. Reflecting on this, I think nothing was by chance, Jesus knows how man's ability tends to over-achieve in all areas, especially language. Words have led to many wars and destruction, both on an individual, local, national, and international levels. He knew we could complicate his instructions, he, therefore, left it simple for our mutual understanding.

Baptize them in the name of the trinity: Father, Son, and Holy Spirit. Again, simple steps to follow, after you have made them disciples, baptize them upon the open profession of their faith and equipping them to follow and now make more disciples. Baptism represents your union in Christ, an outward expression of faith in Christ as demonstrated in the presence of others.

It is an expression of our identification with Christ both on a personal and public level. In *Romans 6:3-4 (NIV)* the Apostle Paul puts it this way: *"Don't you know that all of us who were baptized into Christ were baptized into his death? We were therefore buried with him through baptism into death in order that, just as Christ was raised from the dead through the glory of the Father, we too may live a new life."*

Jesus did not leave the disciples unqualified, because his next instructions were to teach and have them obey God's commands. They were fully prepared to teach others to obey God's commands. This is called a process.

As believers, we need to spend the necessary time to learn Jesus' commands so we can in turn teach others to obey them as well. If we don't know those commands for our living and furthering the Kingdom population, we will not be able to do this part of Jesus' instructions of teaching others to obey.

You might be thinking at this point that you are not a teacher. In our humanistic approach we see a teacher as someone who stands before an audience, has some form of a pulpit, a podium, a synagogue, a preacher/pastor, a college professor might even come to mind. And yes, you would be correct. However, a teacher is anyone who imparts words to someone else to add, share, instruct, and or impart words of understanding to another. In that broader context, we are all teachers. We teach others daily in our written words, conversations, and interactions, especially those non-verbal moments, our body language, including facial expressions, such as a smile. We are therefore all teachers by nature and share our learnings with others.

And there in our non-verbal cues potentially lies some of our challenges. As believers, we are constantly demonstrating the lessons and standards of Christ. The great news is that as we mirror our life after Christ, it becomes habit-forming in our growth and our teaching moments are expressed confidently as we reflect the life of Jesus. We are all on separate journeys in our experiences, as a result, we are not to compare ourselves to the next person, but to prepare ourselves in our desire to draw nearer to Christ. Remember, the Apostle Paul reminds us in *Romans 8:1 (NIV)*: *"Therefore, there is now no condemnation for those who are in Christ Jesus."*

Jesus did not leave us ill-prepared, the final part of the great commission states, Jesus will be with us always, to the end of this age. Meaning He will never abandon us and is always with us, death does not sever our connection to Jesus. Because he overcame death, we do too the minute we accept the gift of salvation.

As a matter of fact, Jesus' death on the cross, did away with eternal separation for all who believe in Him. As believers, we are eternally secure with Him. Now, that is worth sharing with those who are afflicted and cannot see their way through their situation. The hope of no separation from our Creator is worthy of sharing, paying it forward. We are to share the good news of the Gospel of Jesus.

Heaven waits for us, our direction is to bring as many with us as possible. Our assignment is not looking forward to heaven, but to have Gods' will done on earth as it is in heaven. We want those suffering to have the hope of our praising, no matter what they are going through, praise God with our newfound freedom in Him.

One of the talents I wish I were granted was a voice to sing like an angel (What exactly does that mean anyway?). Who has physically heard an angel sing and knows they sound a specific way to our human ears? We probably would run and hide if that were to ever happen, I am even imagining we might even go deaf with the musical octave of their voice. Who knows? Well, those of us who cannot sing, we can dance, clap our hands, stomp our feet, whistle, play an instrument (even air instruments count), the point is to praise and bring our honor to God.

May our praise and worship in singing be like David, who the Bible states danced and sung like he was losing his mind before his God. When so enthralled in those moments David did not care who was present, he worshiped God recklessly. I believe that is one reason God states that David was a man after His heart. I do not know about you, but that is the kind of worship that moves me, the kind that you can feel from the depths of your soul. It reminds me of the phrase in Psalms 42:7 (NIV) that says, "Deep calls to deep in the roar of your waterfalls; all your waves and breakers have swept over me". I imagine my spirit connecting to His Spirit in such intimacy that the Father is pleased, I imagine it being a sweet-smelling aroma to his nostrils, the results of our praise and prayers that moves him. Remember if your prayers do not move yourself, do not expect it to move God. God responds to our heartfelt calls.

To be labeled a man after God's heart is the ultimate acknowledgment from God in my humble opinion. I think that takes a stance for paying it forward and listening to the Holy Spirit direct our steps. While the Holy Spirit helps to direct our steps, we still need to activate our will to do the will of God. As believers it does not mean we no longer have a will, God does not control the will of man. As a result, we intentionally choose to pay it forward to do the will of God.

David has that on lock-down. He was no perfect man, but he wholeheartedly believed in a perfect God and went to him often. Again, he was not perfect by all standards, but his heart was always towards acknowledging his God and depending on Him for direction and guidance.

To be clear, God does not control the will of man, it is ours. There are as many assumptions as possible on 'man's will' versus God's will and who is in control. Some will even venture to say why even bother, God makes the decision for us to enter heaven or hell. Not so! To be fair, both positions bear some element of truth. While God is in control due to the mere fact that He is the creator of everything, God did provide men freewill. We get to decide if we allow God to truly reign in our lives or be self-directed. I believe God provides each of us with the choice for salvation. With that said, we make the choice to be his children versus strictly his creation.

Many of the indecisiveness comes because of habits. We get 'married' to our desires and way of doing things and often encounter difficulties when asked to pivot to an alternate direction. We attempt to justify our methods and in so doing produce the same result yet desiring a different outcome. The word insanity is described in that manner, doing the same thing over and over and expecting a different outcome.

Jesus provides us with a solution. Jesus said to follow him, in so doing we must be willing to take directions from him. And here lies some of our dilemma, we get conflicted in following directions and living by godly standards. We can feel like we are missing out. Again, not so! Following Jesus is setting in motion the plans God has for your life because that is the purpose for which you were created. The beauty of following is just that, we get to follow and not try to take the lead and think we got this now. This is where most of us deviate from the perfect plans of God. Remember he always has the intended 'yes' path for us to follow him.

Following Jesus takes a reset to our psyche, a change from our way to his way. A method of operating that requires renewal, as in a repentant heart. That simply means to change our minds from our old self to a new self, one that requires a reboot. Think of it this way, if you received an old computer that already had programs/software from the original owner and now this computer has been gifted to you, for it to meet your needs, you now must reset the hard drive, clean it up so that the computer can now operate according to your needs.

In like fashion, we turn over our will to take on the will of God for our life, we are in essence resetting (rebooting) our hard drive (our heart) to attend to the will of God. The computer works either way, but does it meet the agenda of the owner if used for a different purpose. Our will works either way, for God or against Him to produce an intended purpose. As followers of Christ; His will is always best for us, he knows the path better than us.

Our heart is controlled by our mind, the mind is the center of the soul, and the battle in life is for the soul of man. It is a hard job involving conversion, which is why we were not left without a helper, the Holy Spirit, God's software. We become what we continuously see, download into our psyche, and therefore must rely on the Holy Spirit for direction and understanding to fulfill the will of God.

The soul which houses our mind, will, and emotions, is the first component of media created by God. It is the mediator between our body and spirit, the soul decides what the body receives, and the devil is after our soul. He cares less about our body and spirit. He manipulates our soul because that is where our senses reside and deposit information into our spirit. We must learn to master our soul by taking heed of the emotions that direct the soul. We must get to a place where we say as David did in *Psalms 42:2 (NIV), "My soul thirsts for God, for the living God. When can I go and meet with God?"*

In *Matthew 16:26 (KJV): "For what is a man profited, if he shall gain the whole world, and lose his own soul? or what shall a man give in exchange for his soul?"* Can we truly be profitable if we have everything the world has to offer and as a result exchanged our soul for it? We cannot serve two masters, God and the world.

How do we pay it forward in our day-to-day living? How do we look back and be grateful for small beginnings and appreciate the wisdom along that journey? These are questions we each need to evaluate and answer from a heart perspective.

If you are reading this book and is likewise curious, the answer is as Jesus told us, to go and make disciples. Look to see where the need is and how you can fill the gap, pay it forward.

You may be asking how to do this. It does not need to be on a grandiose scale but look around you, who needs help? What is the thing you enjoy doing most often and are not being paid to do it? Where and with whom can you share your talents? What local charities can use your 'used' goods? What local charities can use a financial donation? What friend is struggling that you can assist, emotionally, physically, mentally, financially, share a listening ear, an open conversation? Who can you share a meal with and add encouragement to their day? Who can you take a walk with and simply provide a space to their expressions? Who can you send a card to just because you were thinking of them? Who can you send a text/email to just because you were thinking of them? Who can you call because they popped in your thoughts that day? Who can you volunteer your services to without expecting anything in return?

Remember the words of Jesus in *Luke 10:2 (NIV)*, *"He told them, 'The harvest is plentiful', but the workers are few. Ask the Lord of the harvest, therefore, to send out workers into his harvest field."* If you are not sure how to pay it forward, ask the Lord to show you how to use your talent for the betterment of His kingdom. Most of us truly desire to better the world and lives of the people around us, we get deflated because we see it as such an enormous task outside of our skill sets. Imagine the power of one-to-one connections.

Sometimes we need to look directly in front of us to produce the necessary changes we want in our life. We start by looking at our internal inventory, asking the Holy Spirit how to use our talent for the betterment of others. We start somewhere, but the idea is not to remain stagnant and to simply start to pay it forward. This creates the pattern of multiplication and addition into the Kingdom of God and makes more disciples.

Each one learns and adapts accordingly to Jesus' pattern, sometimes he presented in a crowd, but often his interactions were on a one-to-one basis, building relationships. He cares that much for each one of us not only does he hear us, but also sees us.

Think about it, Jesus prepared the way for us before we were even thought of by our parents, what greater love in setting us up for success. His plea is that we share his love, each one reaches another, helping another on their journey in Christ.

Observation Point: Paying it forward is a matter of mindset and habit. As we do learn to give back and consider the next person, we develop habits of meeting the needs of others. We read about this example in the book of Joshua when leading the children of Israel to cross the Jordan. God had given the Promised Land to the children of Israel, but they had to get to it to be granted access to inhabit the land. The tribes of Reuben, Gad and the half-tribe of Manasseh decided they wanted to occupy land prior to crossing the river Jordan because it would be beneficial to their living. God granted their request in the success to occupy the chosen land, but part of that agreement involved assisting the remaining tribes to acquire their territory. God told them, 'for you to be at rest, you must help ensure the rest of your brothers as well.' They had to pay it forward so that everyone could receive the blessings of their land provisions.

Our blessing is dependent on the helping of those less fortunate in the kingdom of God. We are blessed to be a blessing. Paying it forward becomes a habit in the kingdom of God, we are accountable to each other in multiplying the provisions received by God. After all, *Psalm 24:1 (KJV)* reminds us, *" The earth is the* LORD's, *and the fullness thereof;*

the world, and they that dwell therein." In God's kingdom, we are borrowed vessels designed for His glory and honor. Will you be quick to honor Him by paying it forward?

Reader's Notes: *Embrace the Message Within*

CONCLUSION

Our prayer is that you have enjoyed this book as much as we have enjoyed learning, researching, and growing from the small things that God has put on our path, such as these rocks. We challenge you to embrace the messages and encourage you to live your life with your eyes wide open, looking for the *"Unseen Treasures"* that may be awaiting you. As we go through life, we never know what may come. There's pain and sadness, joy and gladness but we must understand that through it all, even though at times it doesn't feel like it, there is a beautiful diamond being created within us. We encourage you to find joy in the simple things as you will never know what insightful experiences are being prepared for you. If something as small as a rock could speak to our hearts, no telling what could speak to yours. God is in the details of our lives; we just have to look for Him.

CPSIA information can be obtained
at www.ICGtesting.com
Printed in the USA
LVHW070552111022
730423LV00009B/127

9 781662 854910